Penguin Books

The Bog Irish

Frank Murphy's paternal ancestors left their
native County Kilkenny for Australia in
1850; on his mother's side he descends from
the O'Canty's, an old bardic family of
Munster. He was born in Leongatha,
Victoria, in 1949. After learning his
catechism at the parish school of St.
Lawrence O'Toole, he matriculated from
St. Patrick's College, Sale, then studied
languages at the Australian National
University. He lived for some time in France,
where he met his wife, and now has four sons.

Young women beetle their washing in a stream

THE BOG IRISH

WHO THEY WERE AND HOW THEY LIVED

edited by
FRANK MURPHY

Penguin Books

Penguin Books Australia Ltd,
487 Maroondah Highway, P.O. Box 257
Ringwood, Victoria 3134, Australia
Penguin Books Ltd,
Harmondsworth, Middlesex, England
Penguin Books,
40 West 23rd Street, New York, N.Y. 10010, U.S.A.
Penguin Books (Canada) Limited,
2801 John Street, Markham, Ontario, Canada L3R 1B4
Penguin Books (N.Z.) Ltd,
182–190 Wairau Road, Auckland 10, New Zealand

First published by Penguin Books Australia, 1987

Copyright © Introduction and Compilation Frank Murphy, 1987

Typeset in Bembo by Dudley E. King, Melbourne
Made and printed in Australia by The Book Printer, Maryborough

CIP

The Bog Irish.

ISBN 0 14 008439 8.

1. Irish — Social life and customs. 2. Irish — Social conditions.
I. Murphy, Frank, 1949– .

305.8′ 9162

Contents

Contents

Introduction

I

In Britain, North America, Australasia and southern Africa, one has only to leaf through a telephone book to find their great-greatgrandchildren. *They* are the bog Irish who left Ireland in the 19th century, the O'Briens, O'Reillys and O'Sullivans, the Walshes and Ryans and Fitzgeralds whose descendants are now far more numerous in the New World than in Ireland itself. Given the poverty and widespread illiteracy of these migrants, it is hardly surprising that their descendants seldom know much of them beyond perhaps their names and the name of the townland or county from which their family came. Fewer still know anything of the distinctive culture of their forebears, or even that when they stepped off their ship in New York or Melbourne, many of them spoke Irish better than English. The object of this book, put simply, is to go back in time and take a closer look at the world of the bog Irish.

This expression – one of a number of pejorative terms which the English language, but no other, has devised for the Irish – does not figure in the Oxford English Dictionary; this gives only *boglanders,* with no reference earlier than 1730. *Bog,* which seems to have entered English in the 16th century, comes from an Irish word meaning *soft* or *yielding.* Land that is bog is generally poor land, to be farmed only when there is no other to be had. In a strict sense then, the bog Irish are precisely that: wretched Irishmen reduced to wringing a wretched livelihood out of wretched soil.

To understand the term fully however, we need to set it in its historical context by tracing the fortunes of the Irish people from the 17th century to the great Famine of 1845–50.

Ireland's history in the 17th century may usefully be compared to that of France in more recent times. In the seventy-five years between 1870 and 1945, France was invaded by German armies on three occasions: in the Franco-Prussian War (1870), in the First World War (1914-18), and in World War II. At each invasion the French people knew the carnage of battle, the humiliation of having the enemy on their soil, the difficult task of rebuilding in the aftermath of war. So too, in the 17th century, the Irish were defeated by the English three times in ninety years: at Kinsale in 1601, then by Cromwell in 1650, and finally in 1690 at the Battle of the Boyne. But there the comparison ends. For whereas the enemy eventually withdrew from France on each occasion – with the exception of Alsace and Lorraine, which were German possessions from 1871 until the end of World War II – the English did not leave Ireland. After each victory they strengthened their hold so that, with gathering momentum, English law, English ways, and above all the English language came to dominate Irish life.

To break the resistance of this irksome people, which it had claimed to govern since the 12th century, the English administration had to crush its ruling class. This comprised two groups that had originally been quite distinct: on the one hand were the Old English, the often Hibernicised descendants of earlier Anglo-Norman invaders, and on the other the powerful Gaelic chieftains. Both these groups opposed English rule, and their common badge, in a period when the English sought to impose Protestant modes of worship, was their fierce Catholicism. Extending a policy which they had begun in the 16th century, the English undermined these groups by the simple expedient of confiscating the land on which their power depended, and giving it over to *planters* or settlers who became known as the New English. The original occupiers were often forced to move to inferior lands or bogs, becoming literally *bog Irish*. In the massive confiscations, evictions and redistributions of the 17th century, only one group in Ireland did not suffer, namely the new ruling class, which was almost exclusively English-speaking and Protestant. Hence, from the 17th century on, the term *bog Irish* may be taken to signify the majority of the population, generally rural, Irish-speaking and Catholic. This broader meaning is the one understood in this book.

Whether literally or figuratively, no-one in Ireland wanted to be forced into the bogs, least of all those who had most to lose. The pressure of English rule was such, however, that to avoid being *déclassé*, the Irish, particularly those who belonged to the old Catholic nobility or gentry, had only two means of escape. They could conform to the established (Anglican) church, as many did; or they could take what seemed to many the more honourable course, and emigrate. Throughout the 17th and 18th centuries countless Irishmen fled to the Continent, where they were to be found shriving Catholic penitents, tutoring the heirs to Catholic thrones, curing Catholic illnesses and riding into battle for Catholic kings. At the end of the 17th century there were twenty thousand Irish soldiers in the French army. Their valour was legendary: Ireland's best and bravest blood stained the battlefields of Europe.

One could be forgiven for thinking that just as their class was doomed, so they too showed a sort of death wish. Some would see this hypothesis confirmed by the two professions they commonly followed, soldiering and the priesthood, both of which reduced their chances of leaving any descendants. On the other hand, it might be argued, what else could their class do? At least on the Continent they could use their talents as befitted their origins; but not so in Ireland. There, under the Penal Laws designed to break the Irish Catholic landed class, they were barred from the professions, from voting and from all public office; when a Catholic died his estate had to be broken up by being shared equally among his children; no Catholic might bear arms or keep a horse worth more than five pounds. Between 1641 and 1697, to take one example, the number of Catholic landowners in County Wexford fell from 152 to none. The little land still remaining in Catholic hands at the end of the 17th century passed from its owners, almost without exception, in the early part of the 18th century. It was in the 17th century, as a result of this contest for possession of Ireland, that the notions *Irish* and *Catholic* became one, to Irish Catholics at least, few of whom had <u>not</u> been reduced to the status of bog Irish.

It is a rare Irishman who does not know his country's history in one form or another. And those who sailed to the Continent in this period must have likened themselves as they left their native land to their celebrated countrymen Hugh O'Neill and Rory O'Donnell, whose going into exile is one of the Great Moments in Irish history. Earl of Tyrone and Earl of Tyrconnel respectively, they had unsuccessfully fought against the English before leaving Ireland forever, together with their families and friends. Tradition has it that as their ship drew away from the shores of Lough Swilly at midnight on 14th September 1607, taking with it the shattered hopes of the Irish, 'a great cry of lament and farewell went up from their followers left behind upon the shore'.* Robin Flower has translated from the Irish these lines written by Aindrais MacMarcuis, a poet of the time:

> This night sees Eire desolate,
> Her chiefs are cast out of their state;
> Her men, her maidens weep to see
> Her desolate that should peopled be . . .
>
> Man after man, day after day
> Her noblest princes pass away

---

* Robin Flower, *The Irish Tradition*, Oxford University Press, 1979 edition. Unless otherwise specified the quotations in this introduction are taken from pp. 166-171 of this book.

And leave to all the rabble rest
A land dispeopled of her best . . .

Woe to the Gael in this sore plight!
Henceforth they shall not know delight.
No tidings now their woe relieves,
Too close the gnawing sorrow cleaves.

These the examples of their woe:
Israel in Egypt long agó,
Troy that the Greek hosts set on flame,
And Babylon that to ruin came.

Sundered from hope, what friendly hand
Can save the sea-surrounded land?
The clan of Conn no Moses see
To lead them from captivity.

Her chiefs are gone. There's none to bear
Her cross or lift her from despair;
The grieving lords take ship. With these
Our very souls pass overseas.

That MacMarcuis should regret the 'grieving lords' is scarcely surprising, for he was a poet or, as we would say, a member of the intelligentsia. Poets in traditional Irish society were closely allied to the aristocracy on whom they depended for patronage: the poet in return sang the praises of his prince, often literally. As was also the case for medicine and the law, the practice of poetry was usually reserved to certain families whose surnames often reflected their literary calling: O'Clery (from *cléireach*, a clerk); O'Canty (from *cáinteach*, a satirist); Ward or Macaward (from the word *bárd*), to take a few examples. Most illustrious of these poetic families were the O'Dalys, who were prominent in Irish letters from the 12th to the 17th century, and claimed to descend from Dalach, a 7th-century disciple of St Colman. One would expect the poets to be conservative in outlook given their social origins, their links with the aristocracy and their pedantic schooling. And so they generally were. Nonetheless, as the keepers of Ireland's past glories and the heirs to what is said to be the oldest literature in Europe after those of Greece and Rome, they had, for all their faults, good reason to pride themselves on the central part they played in maintaining the distinctive traditions of their country.

But powerful as they seemed, their power rested on a fragile base, and when the old landed class fell so did they. There is a story that a poet called MacBrodin was killed by being thrown from a cliff by a Cromwellian soldier who shouted after him as he fell down, 'Sing your rann now, little man!' No doubt this is an extreme case, but in the late 17th and early 18th centuries, as they never cease to remind us, their lot was not an easy one. From being a privileged class they were brought down to the status of cottiers or labourers. 'Here I am in hunger and thirst,' wrote David O'Bruadair (1625-98), 'a lonely labourer wielding a tool that I was not used to in my days of fullness. My knuckles are all swollen from the motion of the clay-spade, and its handle has completely ruined my fingers.'

The Irish language itself fared no better, especially after 1746 when, with the collapse of the Jacobite cause, it became clear to those who spoke it that they could no more rid themselves of the English tongue than of English rule. Abandoned by the upper classes, it retreated both geographically (westwards) and socially (downwards) throughout the 18th century. Gaelic culture ceased to be aristocratic: its custodians were now the peasantry. Huddled over the turf-fire, deeming themselves lucky if they had buttermilk on their potatoes, they saw English as the language of the *Teach Mór* or Big House, the new Palladian mansions in which the landlords drank claret, gambled and exchanged ideas on how to rid the district of Whiteboys, one of several secret societies born of peasant discontent.

Language was not the only thing which distinguished their masters from the great mass of the people: there was also the ubiquitous religious question. If the piety of the Irish was real, their rejection of English authority was no less so. The government for its part was suspicious of the Church of Rome, fearing that it would weaken the State. In the early part of the 18th century it was still trying to suppress the influence of the Church in various ways. Among other measures it forbade any form of Catholic education in Ireland, which meant that young men intending to be priests had to study in Irish colleges on the Continent. The spirit of this bitter period may be judged from this section of a letter which the Irish Privy Council sent to London on 27th August 1719:

Priests, Friars etc. are no sooner transported but new ones come over from France, Spain or Portugal, so that their number continues as great as ever. The common Irish will never become Protestants or well affected to the Crown while they are supplied with Priests, Friars etc. who are the fomenters and disturbers here. So that some more effectual remedy to prevent Priests and Friars coming into this kingdom is necessary. The [Irish] Commons proposed the marking of every Priest who shall be convicted of being an unregistered Priest, Friar etc. and of remaining in this kingdom after the 1st of May 1720 with a large P to be made with a red hot Iron on the cheek. The [Privy] Council generally disliked that punishment, and have altered it into that of castration which they are persuaded will be the most effectual remedy that can be found out to clear this nation of the disturbers of the peace and quiet of the kingdom.*

Saner counsels prevailed, fortunately, and neither of these extreme punishments ever came into force even in the worst years of the Penal Laws. As the century progressed, the Government and the Church hierarchy reached a *modus vivendi* whereby the Government tolerated the bishops but expected them in return to help keep the peace. Irish though they might have been, the bishops and many of the lesser clergy generally came from a social background which helped them to see the importance of preaching deference to the established order of things, albeit a Protestant one, and in any case they were grateful for whatever concessions they could have. This co-

---

* Rev. William P. Burke, *The Irish Priests in the Penal Times 1660-1760*, N. Harvey & Co., Waterford, 1914, pp. 200-201.

operation proving fruitful to both sides, at the end of the century the Government set up the seminary of Maynooth, which it endowed. For all their differences, both the hierarchy and the Government agreed that it was better to allow future priests to study in Ireland where they could be watched, than in France where they might imbibe the ideas of the Revolution.

As this changed climate in the relations between Church and State reveals, the English Government found that in order to function, it had to deal with leaders in whom the Irish people had some confidence. Having got rid of the old ruling class, it had no alternative but the princes of a Church which it loathed. Hence, as has been noted, if the Irish became a priest-ridden people, this was largely a direct consequence of English colonial policy. But the new climate also meant that priests now preached their sermons in English, not Irish. Thus, in coming to terms with English rule, the Church proved to be one of the most effective instruments of anglicisation, helping its former persecutor to undermine the indigenous language and culture of the Irish people. The money the English spent on educating 'Romish' priests proved to be one of the soundest investments they ever made in Ireland.

At the beginning of the 19th century Irish was still the usual language of half the Irish people, although few could read it. Anthony Raftery, the last major poet to use Irish before its modern revival, died in 1835; Humphrey O'Sullivan, the Kilkenny schoolmaster whose diary in Irish gives a rare insight into pre-Famine life, in 1838. The establishment of English-medium national schools helped to shorten its agony. When the potato famine began in 1845, it struck hardest at the poorest sections of the population, which had the highest proportion of Irish-speakers. Through starvation, disease and emigration the population fell quickly from about eight and a half million on the eve of the Famine to six and a half million in 1851. According to the census taken in that year, a quarter of the people could speak Irish, but

Ireland in the early 1840s

only five per cent were monolingual speakers. The Irish in those desperate years had more to worry about than the death of their language, and with it perhaps the greater part of their Irishness.

The exhausted and very different Ireland that emerged from the Famine is beyond the scope of this book, which concentrates on the bog or common Irish in the period when they were the chief keepers of their country's ancient culture and still spoke Irish. This period begins in the middle of the 17th century and ends with the Famine. Though subtitled 'A Portrait of the Native or Common Irish', the book is largely their self-portrait, as I have thought it best to let the people of the time speak for themselves through contemporary documents as far as possible. It must be remembered that few people could read or write, and that those who could were rarely interested in the doings of humble folk. The texts have been chosen for what they tell of Irish life and are grouped according to theme. Explanations and notes have been kept to the minimum necessary for understanding. Although some of the texts translated from Irish may seem strange, and at times even difficult, I have not hesitated to give preference to documents written in that tongue. Those I have translated fall short of the originals but convey, I hope, something of their spirit.

II

As anyone who has visited Lourdes can testify, the Irish are incorrigible pilgrims. The German writer Walafrid Strabo noted their wanderlust as early as the 9th century, while Donnchadh Mór Ó Dálaigh (1175–1244), a member of the O'Daly family mentioned above, took as the subject for one of the best-known religious poems in Irish the idea of a pilgrimage to Lough Derg in County Donegal. Closer to our own time, in his *Traits and Stories of the Irish Peasantry* (1830-33), William Carleton tells how in his day those who made the daunting pilgrimage to this same place would bring back little bags of pebbles from the lake as a gift for their families and friends. It is difficult not to compare them to the flasks of water which their descendants now bring back from Lourdes, as Carleton says that 'an uncommon virtue in curing all kinds of complaints' was ascribed to them. As he distributed his little stones the pilgrim doubtless recalled all the wonderful things he had seen on his travels, and attempted to share his experience with those who for one reason or another could not make the journey. Humble as they were, he was proud of his pebbles, which came from Lough Derg itself.

Like those pebbles, this book on the bog Irish has humble origins. Three years ago, while making up a family tree, I felt the need to know more about my forebears than their names and dates of birth: I wanted to have some idea of everyday Irish life before the Famine, and above all to enter that part of my family's past which was hidden from me because I had no Irish. To appease my curiosity I had first to learn to read the language. Then as I studied what books I could find, in English or Irish, I took note of illustrations or texts which sharpened my understanding of the old Irish world. At the back of my mind was the idea that, photocopied, they would be of interest to my family as background material for a family history. As I uncovered more and more material, much of it from books that are now rare, I realised that it was outgrowing my original intention and transforming itself into a book: such a book, it seemed, would be useful as it would bring together a range of texts that might otherwise be inaccessible to many.

But if this book is like the pilgrim's pebbles in having humble origins, it differs from them in that it has no magical or miraculous properties. It is the work of an amateur family historian; it is necessarily subjective; it makes no claim to be definitive or exhaustive. Such as it is, however, I offer it as a keepsake through which others may share in what was, for me, a pilgrimage.

FRANK MURPHY MELBOURNE, 1986

Note: A glossary of Irish words and phrases is given at the end of the book.

PRINCES AND POETS

Cnéad í an anḃnainn-ṛe aṛ Éiṛinn?
Nó cnéad daṁna a daoiṛ-ẓeiḃinn?
Iniṛ cṛann-ṛuad na ṛéad ṛean,
Cnéad an ṫ-aṁluad ṛá'ṛ ḣaiṛẓead?

> Why does Ireland falter?
> What is the cause of her bondage?
> Isle of brown trees, ancient jewel,
> Wherefore this desolation?
> GEOFFREY O'DONOGHUE (c.1675)

At the close of the 17th century Ireland was a nation in ruins. With its sacked and burned buildings the landscape bore (and still bears) witness to the wars of the past century; the old institutions and structures were breaking down; the invader could not be dislodged. In the following decades the Irish people came to terms with the new order as best they could. But even as the old Gaelic world slowly died, their poets reminded them of it unremittingly.

A Visit to the O'Flahertys

From the time when the Anglo-Normans first came to Ireland in
1169, the great clans made government difficult. One of the
most warlike was that of the O'Flahertys, who struck such fear into
the inhabitants of medieval Galway that they engraved on one
of their city gates the prayer 'From the fury of the O'Flahertys,
deliver us O Lord'. The name itself contains the Irish word *flaith*
(ruler, lord): no doubt the writer Liam O'Flaherty had this in mind
when he said that his surname was 'the only princely thing' that
he had. One senses the same pride of race, of being an O Flaith-
bheartaigh, in this account written by an Englishman at the end
of the 17th century.

A gentleman in Galway to whom I was recommended by one
who was friend to us both in Dublin gave me his recommendato-
rye letters to one O'Flaghertie the most considerable man in this
territorye. He was son to one Sir Murragh na Mart O Flaghertie;
the name of na Mart was added uppon the occasion of his killing
and devoureing in his one house, among his servants and followers everye Shrove Tuesday at night fifty beefes, and this I am told
of the Irish papists in generall that the eve of their Lent they doe
lay in a great deale of flesh, gormandizeing that night enough to
serve them untill Easter, at which time they rise early in the
morning to swallow down more of their beloved flesh; but this
you must take notice of in the vulgar and poorer sort of people,
not among the gentry. This gentlemen was among a greate
company of his relations, as being the chiefe of the clan or family,
when I arrived at his house, which was a long cabbin, the walls of
hurdles plaister'd with cow dung and clay. I produced my creden-
tialls and was civilly received. They were a parcell of tall lusty
fellows with long hair, straite and well made, only clumsy in
their leggs, theire ankles thicker in proportion to their calves
than the English, which is attributed to theire weareing broags

without any heels; but this I leave to the learned. The men after the old Irish fashion as well as the weomen weore theire haire verie long, as an ornament, and to add to it the weomen commonly on Saturday night, or the night before they make their appearance at mass or any publick meeting doe wash it in a lee made with stale urine and ashes, and after in water to take away the smell, by which their locks are of a burnt yellow colour much in vogue among them . . .

There was a mutton killed for supper, half of which was boyl'd and the other roasted, and all devour'd at the meale. After supper the priest, who as I suppose was a sort of chaplaine to the family called for tables to play for an half-pennorth of tobacco, but was reprimanded by the lady of the house for doeing it before he had return'd thanks, and civilly enquired of me if I understood the game. My being ignorant of it made them lay it aside. I made the priest a present of my tobacco which was wellcome to them all; even the lady herself bore them company in smoakeing and excus'd it by urgeing the need they were in of some such thing in that moist country, which I could not contradict. I enquired about the customs of ploweing by their horses tayl, and burning the corn in the straw. They told me the former was wholly disused as a thing too injurious, their cattle often loosing their tayls thereby, but they still burn their corn to save themselves the trouble of thrashing, soe that in one houres time you may see the sheaves taken out of the stack and burnt, the corn winnowed ground on theire querns and made bread for the table . . .

Quern or handmill for grinding corn

The house was one entire long room without any partition. In the middle of it was the fire place with a large wood fire which was no way unpleaseing tho in summer time. It had no chimney but a vent hole for the smoake at the ridge, and I observed the people here much troubled with sore eyes; which I attributed to the sharp smoak of the wood, and they also allowed it but sayd they had newly put this up for a Booley or summer habitation, the proper dwelling or mansion house being some miles farther neare the sea, and such an one they commonly built everie yeare in some one place or other, and thatch'd it with rushed or coarse grass as this was; we all lay in the same roome upon green rushes. I had sheets and soft white blankets which they emulate one another in verie much (I meane the housewives among them), and they assur'd me no man ever gott cold by lyeing on green rushes, which indeed are sweet and cleane, being changed everie day if raine hinders not; but tho they have not lice among them, they are verie full of white snayles which I found upon my cloaths. I wonder'd mightily to hear people walking to the fire place in the middle of the house to piss there in the ashes, but I was soone after forced to doe soe too for want of a chambrepot, which they are not much used unto . . .

The next morning earely after a large breakefast of six wodden bowls filled with hott flesh meate which I could not taste, and a drachm of theire bulcaan or worse sort of aqua vitae, Offlaghertie invited me to walk a small mile to view theire deer. I willingly consented because I did not expect to heare of Deer Park in so wild a place; we walked over mountains and through boogs, thro thick and thin, sometimes out and sometimes in untill I lost the heels of my shoes, which tyred me soe that I thought I should never come to the miles end, which was modestly speakeing as farr as half way from Whitehall to Barnet. At last we came to a pleasant vale called Glinglass, or the Green Vale, of an English miles breadth encompasst with lovely green mountains which were tufted with pleasant groves and thickets of natures providing, for none here imitate her in ought but her coarser draughts; on the sides of these hills I wonder'd to see some hundreds of stately red deer, the stags bigger than a large English yeareling calfe, with suitable antlers much bigger than any I ever saw before.

It was the most pleaseing scene that ever I met with in this kingdom, and the only thing worth my notice in these parts. We return'd before the heate of the day to our greate cabbin, where we had at dinner, no less than a whole beef boyl'd and roasted, and what mutton I know not so profewsly did they lay it on the table. At the upper end where the lady sate was placed an heap of oaten cakes about a foot high, such another in the middle and the like at the lower end; at each side of the middle heap were placed two large vessells filled with Troander or the whey made with buttermilk and sweet milk, which being about two days old was wonderfull cold and pleaseing in that hott time of the day. We had ale (such as it was) and Bulcaan, and after dinner myn host ordered his doggs to be gotten ready to hunt the stagg.

JOHN DUNTON, *Teague Land, or a Merry Ramble to the Wild Irish,* 1698

O'Rourke's Feast

The subject of this poem is a 16th-century chieftain of the O'Rourkes. The Leitrim author of the Irish original, Hugh McGauran, gave an English translation of it to Jonathan Swift, who used it as a basis for this rendering.

1

O'Rourke's noble fare
Will ne'er be forgot,
By those who were there,
And those who were not.
His revels to keep,
We sup and we dine,
On seven score sheep,
Fat bullocks and swine.

Madder: traditional drinking vessel

Usquebagh to our feast
  In pails was brought up,
A hundred at least,
  And a madder our cup.
O there is the sport,
  We rise with the light,
In disorderly sort,
  From snoring all night.
O how was I trick't,
  My pipe it was broke,
My pocket was pick't,
  I lost my new cloak.
I'm rifled, quoth Nell,
  Of mantle and kercher.
Why then fare thee well,
  The de'il take the searcher.
Come harper, strike up,
  But first by your favour,
Boy, give us a cup:
  Ay, this has some savour.

2

O'Rourke's jolly boys
  Ne'er dream't of the matter,
Till rowz'd by the noise,
  And musical clatter,
They bounce from their nest,
  No longer will tarry,
They rise ready drest,
  Without one Ave Mary.
They dance in a round,
  Cutting capers and ramping,
A mercy the ground
  Did not burst with their stamping.

The floor is all wet
  With leaps and with jumps,
While the water and sweat,
  Splish, splash in their pumps.
Bless you late and early,
  Laughlin O Enagin,
By my hand, you dance rarely,
  Margery Grinagin.
Bring straw for our bed,
  Shake it down to the feet,
Then over us spread
  The winnowing sheet.
To show I don't flinch,
  Fill the bowl up again,
Then give us a pinch
  Of your sneezing: a yean.

3

Good Lord, what a sight,
  After all their good cheer,
For people to fight,
  In the midst of their beer:
They rise from their feast,
  And hot are their brains;
A cubit at least
  The length of their skeans.
What stabs and what cuts,
  What clatt'ring of sticks,
What strokes on the guts,
  What bastings and kicks!
With cudgels of oak
  Well hardened in flame,
A hundred heads broke,
  A hundred struck lame.

*Glass that had
to be emptied before
being put back
on the table*

You churle, I'll maintain
  My father built Lusk,
The castle of Slain,
  And Carrickdrumrusk:
The Earl of Kildare,
  And Moynalta, his brother,
As great as they are,
  I was nurs'd by their mother.
Ask that of old madam,
  She'll tell you who's who,
As far up as Adam,
  She knows it is true.
Come down with that beam,
  If cudgels are scarce,
A blow on the weam,
  Or a kick on the arse.

Version by JONATHAN SWIFT (1667–1745)
After the Irish of Hugh McGauran, c.1720

The Woman of Three Cows

Petty class distinctions existed at all levels of Irish society. The translator of this ballad notes that it was intended 'as a rebuke to a woman in humble life, who assumed airs of consequence from being the possessor of three cows'.

O Woman of Three Cows, a-gradh!
  don't let your tongue thus rattle!
O don't be saucy, don't be stiff,
  because you may have cattle,
I have seen – and here's my hand to you,
  I only say what's true –
A many a one with twice your stock
  not half as proud as you.

Good luck to you, don't scorn the poor,
   and don't be their despiser;
For worldly wealth soon melts away,
   and cheats the very miser:
And death soon strips the proudest wreath
   from haughty human brows,
Then don't be stiff, and don't be proud,
   good Woman of Three Cows!

See where Momonia's heroes lie,
   proud Owen More's descendants,
'Tis they that won the glorious name,
   and had the grand attendants,
If *they* were forced to bow to Fate,
   as every mortal bows,
Can *you* be proud, can *you* be stiff,
   my Woman of Three Cows?

The brave sons of the Lord of Clare,
   they left the land to mourning;
Mo bhrón! for they were banished,
   with no hope of their returning –
Who knows in what abodes of want
   those youths were driven to house?
Yet *you* can give yourself these airs,
   O Woman of Three Cows!

O think of Donnell of the ships,
   the Chief whom nothing daunted –
See how he fell in distant Spain,
   unchronicled, unchaunted!
He sleeps, the great O'Sullivan,
   where thunder cannot rouse –
Then ask yourself, should *you* be proud,
   good Woman of Three Cows!

O'Ruark, Maguire, those souls of fire,
    whose names are shrined in story –
Think how their high achievements once
    made Erin's greatest glory –
Yet now their bones lie mouldering
    under weeds and cypress boughs,
And so, for all your pride, will yours,
    O Woman of Three Cows!

The O'Carrolls, also, famed when fame
    was only for the boldest,
Rest in forgotten sepulchres
    with Erin's best and oldest;
Yet who so great as they of yore
    in battle or carouse?
Just think of that, and hide your head,
    good Woman of Three Cows!

Your neighbour's poor, and you, it seems,
    are big with vain ideas,
Because, an eadh! you've got three cows,
    one more, I see, than *she* has;
That tongue of yours wags more at times
    than charity allows –
But, if you're strong, be merciful,
    great Woman of Three Cows!

The Summing-Up
Now, there you go! You still, of course,
    keep up your scornful bearing,
And I'm too poor to hinder you;
    but, by the cloak I'm wearing,
If I had but *four* cows myself,

even though you were my spouse,
I'd thwack you well to cure your pride,
my Woman of Three Cows!

Anon. 17th century
Trans. JAMES CLARENCE MANGAN

On the Death of O'Callaghan Who Died at Threshertown, Co. Cork, on 24th August 1724

The following is part of an elegy on Daniel O'Callaghan who was in his day *The O'Callaghan*, the chief of his clan, and held sway over some 50000 acres of land. When members of great families died, so it was believed, a *síbhean* or fairy-woman was heard keening the dead person; another form of this word, *bean sí*, gives the English *banshee*. In these lines Egan O'Rahilly describes the *síbhean* of the O'Callaghan family telling of life in the chieftain's household. She celebrates his wealth, his culture and above all his munificence. O'Rahilly lived through the period when a new social class, English-speaking and Protestant, was taking the place of the old aristocracy, Catholic and Irish-speaking, on whose patronage poets like himself depended for their livelihood. He makes no attempt to hide his nostalgia for the old order.

I saw, said she, in his kingly, musical mansion,
Coloured silks, and cloth of pure satin,
Swords being burnished, invalids drinking mead,
And warriors playing at the chess-board.

Coverlets being laid for guests, morning and evening,
Fairhaired maidservants adjusting pillows,
Newly opened wine being quaffed, and high spirits,
Meat on spits, and whiskey on tables.

Guests thronging to the house in fashion,
Guests falling and feverish,
Guests tipsy but not offensive,
Guests discoursing loudly.

Airs being played pleasantly on the harp,
Histories being read by the wise and learned
Which treat without fault of the clergy,
And of every great family that arose in Europe.

Doors wide open onto amber towers,
Candles blazing from every wall and chamber,
Wine-casks being broached for the company at every moment,
And the drink flowing without ebb.

Steeds being offered to the master-poets of Fódla,
Strong horses in teams racing on the hillsides,
Footsoldiers in combat, and much beer,
In goblets wrought from the purest of silver.

Often in the meadows was heard the sound of war-bugles,
The cry of hunters on the misty hillsides,
Foxes being roused for them, and red-bucks,
Hares from the fen, water-hens and thrushes.

Birds of the chase starting up in great numbers,
Pheasant-hens screeching as they disperse,
The prince's hounds and his men weary
From racing up the misty hillsides.

Oh pain without relief! and great sorrow to me,
The meadow rings now to the sound of the jackdaws,
Loud sounds the voice of foreigners in the golden mansion,
Where once there was playing and talking of comrades.

EGAN O'RAHILLY (c.1675–1729)
Trans. FRANK MURPHY

There Are Problems for George

Even after the defeat of Prince Charles Edward Stuart at Culloden in 1746, many Irishmen continued to look to the Continent for help against the English. These lines, which date perhaps from 1778 or 1779, and show the poet anticipating the liberation of Ireland, are here translated literally.

There are problems for George,
  Though great his might on sea;
And Eire will not lighten his task,
  Powerful though his army may be.
Against him the Emperor grows stronger,
  And leads a merry dance.
His force will be spent,
  And his councils frustrated.
Frenchmen and Spaniards are thriving,
  With no favour, affection or pity for him.
And they will make the evil rogue
  Run from the crown with their swords.

Count d'Estaing is an enemy to him,
  And he is on good terms with Charles;
Russia turned a hand with him,
  And will not love him till death.
Many soldiers will come
  Bravely into England,
And they will overcome the English
  With the grace of the Son of God.
We can state boldly:
  Scotland will be covered with white camps,
And we will destroy all the coward's villains,
  No matter how strong their troops and forces.

Good news is running
  Through the provinces of Banbha,

Kinsale in the 18th century

That everyone in Europe
  And their brave forces
Are thrusting at George
  And his sails out on the sea.
However great his strength and hope,
  His armies are in danger.
All will be well again in Whitehall,
  In Ireland and Scotland:
They will destroy the wretched troops who speak English
  Wherever they may be.

Long have the poor Gaels been waiting
  For the fulfilment of each prophecy,
And shortly, without delay, everything
  Will be as they wish;

Every foreign pirate
  Who is sitting in the mansions of Banbha
Will be scattered about,
  Banished far away.
Every brave hero of Irish descent,
  Valiant in deeds and mountain battles,
No matter what ordeal he undergoes
  Will be unharmed (?).

This then is the story
  And all of it true,
That mighty is the *Invasion* [in English in the text]
  Venturing in joy,
Coming to Scotland and Eire
  And to England;
And the warriors of the vigorous race
  Of Milesius [the native Irish] from Spain
Giving rout to the enemy hosts
  And the harbours will blaze with them.
No mercy then for the rogues:
  They will be subdued and brought down.

The Prince, the Crowned One,
  As it is said,
In answer to so many prayers
  Will triumph in the three kingdoms;
Help that is more than middling
  He is getting, and the Empire,
And the forces of Louis,
  Yield in no circumstance;
Armies will come from Spain,
  Proud, strong, warlike;
Destruction, ruin, spoliation, death
  They will make of the swarthy English.

OWEN ROE O'SULLIVAN (1748–1784)
Trans. FRANK MURPHY

Letter from a Collegian

Throughout the 18th century, Irish Catholic families who could afford to do so sent their sons to be educated on the Continent, where there were several well-established Irish colleges. One of the most famous to be educated in this manner was Daniel O'Connell (1785-1847), whose family, like others of the old upper class, had strong connections with the Continent in this period: they grew rich through smuggling, for example, and one of Daniel's uncles was the last Colonel of the Irish Brigade in France. Daniel was sixteen years old when he wrote this letter from his school in the north of France to another uncle, Maurice 'Hunting Cap' O'Connell, the head of the family.

St. Omer: Feb. 3rd, 1792.

My dear Uncle,

Since I had the pleasure of hearing from you last, I received a letter from my Uncle in Paris: he desired us learn mathematicks, logick and rhetoric; as soon as I received his letter, I went to the President to inform him of it; he told me that the price of learning the mathematicks here is a Guinea a month, upon which I wrote to my Uncle to let him know the President's answer. I also told him that if he wished we should follow that system of Education, it would be better send us elsewhere, where we may go thro' a regular course of studies. Not that I find the smallest fault with this Colledge, where every thing that is taught in it is sufficiently attended to; the boys taken very good care of, and the living good enough.

In this Colledge are taught the Latin and Greek authors, French, English, and Geography, besides lessons given during recreation hours in Music, Dancing, Fencing and Drawing. I have not yet enquired about rhetoric, but will do it (please God) as soon as I receive an answer from my Uncle.

We have composed for the second time since I came here. I got second in Latin, Greek and English, and eleventh in French; before the places are read out there is a scene or two of play acted on a small

*Count Daniel O'Connell (1745–1833), last
colonel of the Irish Brigade*

stage, which is in the Colledge, by one of the four first schools (each
in its turn); these they call Orations, and of them there are eight in
the year. Of consequence we compose eight times; there is a whole
play acted in the month of August.

As our trunk was too large to get into our dormitory, we were
obliged to get a small wooden box from the Procurator, nailed
against the wall of the play yard; these are here called houses, we
keep in it the books and other little things we brought with us. The
President told me that he would give the £10 we brought here to
the Procurator to be given to us at the rate of 6d. ster. a fortnight.

I should not mention these particulars but that I thought you

The Irish College of Louvain in the 17th century

would be pleased at our letting you know every circumstance that may happen, therefore we are resolved not to let any slip unnoticed.

I have just received your affectionate letter and return you sincere thanks for it. We hope, my dear Uncle, to be able to shew our gratitude by our ready obedience to all your commands, and by our application to our studies. I have delivered your letter to the Procurator, who receives the boys' pension. I remain, my dear Uncle,

Your affectionate and dutiful Nephew,
Danl. O'Connell

An Answer to Thomas Barry

While a few families managed, like the O'Connells, to keep something of their lands by a mixture of cunning and good fortune, most were ruined by the Penal Laws. Pierce Fitzgerald, who inherited the remnants of a great estate, conformed to the Church of Ireland in order to save his family's last acres. For this he was attacked in verse by a poet of Clonmel, a certain Thomas Barry. Fitzgerald then wrote this reply.

Dearest Barry
My clever friend,
Going over to Calvin
Is my cross to carry
Because my children's loss
Of acres and herds
Left my life a stormy
Heartstream of tears.

Too long has this wrong
Lain on our chiefs.
They are rent, impoverished
And crushed into weakness.
Bright God, if you don't trample
On these foreign boors
Soon all our landowners
Will follow my sad move.

This is a sickness and hurt
Wounding me, never
Ceasing cutting to
My lungs and my liver,
That rather than my children
Be sunk in the dirt

I drew strife on my soul
For love of earth.

Do not harbor anger
In your minds for me,
Enough that Heaven's wrath
Is launched, my friends,
And to guard my soul
I urge the Son of God;
Though I am a sinner
Sunk in the world's mire,
Fettered in the world's chains,
Still to the mild nurse
Of Christ I cry
'Dispel my sighs,
Relieve me of this curse!'

My faith has done me harm
In a way that is not fitting,
And to avoid it for land
Cannot be a proper thing,
I claim it is unfair
And pray now without fail
For help from the unchanging King.

O dear friend, remember
I was a creature cornered,
Though to your mind
Merely a man deluded,
But fines and rent and tax
And costs of litigation
Made many more than me
Cross the road to Luther.

PIERCE FITZGERALD (1709–1791)
Trans. JOAN KEEFE

A Bardic School

Written at a time when they had almost entirely vanished, this description nonetheless gives a good idea of the old Bardic Schools.

The Poetical Seminary, or School . . . was open only to such as were descended from Poets, and reputed within their Tribes: And so it was with all the Schools of that kind in the Nation, being equal to the Number of Families that followed the same Calling: But some more or less frequented for the Difference of Professors, Conveniency, with other Reasons, and seldom any come but from remote Parts, to be at a distance from Relations, and other Acquaintance, that might interrupt his Study. The Qualifications first requir'd, were reading well, writing the Mother-tongue, and a strong Memory. It was likewise necessary the Place should be in the solitary Recess of a Garden, or within a Sept or Inclosure, far out of the reach of any Noise, which an Intercourse of People might otherwise occasion. The Structure was a snug, low Hut, and Beds in it at convenient Distances, each within a small Apartment, without much Furniture of any kind, save only a Table, some Seats, and a Conveniency for Cloaths to hang upon. No Windows to let in the Day, nor any Light at all us'd but that of Candles, and these brought in at a proper Season only. The Students upon thorough Examination being first divided into Classes; wherein a regard was had to every ones Age, Genius, and the Schooling had before, if any at all, or otherwise. The Professors (one or more as there was occasion) gave a Subject suitable to the Capacity of each Class, determining the Number of Rimes, and clearing what was to be chiefly observ'd therein as to Syllables, Quatrans, Concord, Correspondence, Termination, and Union, each of which were restrain'd by peculiar Rules. The said Subject (either one or more as aforesaid) having been given over Night, they work'd it apart each by himself upon his own Bed, the whole next Day in the Dark, till at a certain Hour in the

Night, Lights being brought in, they committed it to writing. Being afterwards dress'd and come together into a large Room, where the Masters waited, each Scholar gave in his Performance, which being corrected or approv'd of (according as it requir'd) either the same or fresh Subjects were given against the next Day. This Part being over, the Students went up to their Meal, which was then serv'd up; and so, after some time spent in Conversation, and other Diversions, each retir'd to his Rest, to be ready for the Business of the next Morning. Every Saturday, and on the Eves of Festival Days, they broke up, and dispers'd themselves among the Gentlemen and rich Farmers of the Country, by whom they were well entertained, and made much of, till they thought fit to take their Leaves, in order to resume their Study. Nor was the People satisfied with affording this Hospitality alone: they sent in by turns every Week from far and near, Liquors, and all manner of Provision towards the Subsistence of the Academy; so that the Chief Poet was at little or no Charges, but on the contrary got very well by it, besides the Presents made him by the Students, upon their first coming, which was always at Michaelmas; and from thence till the 25th of March, during the cold Season of the Year only, did that close Study last. At that time the Scholars broke up, and repair'd each to his own Country, with an Attestation of his Behaviour and Capacity, from the Chief Professor to those that sent him.

Memoirs of the Marquis of Clanrickarde, 1772

Portrait of a Poet

Irish poets of this period were noted for their malice and their wrangling. The following lines, a description of Egan O'Rahilly (c.1675-1729), are by a minor poet of his time. The Irish text is very obscure in places, and Rev. Patrick Dinneen, whose literal translation is given below, admits that in some places it is 'merely tentative'. But the poet's meaning is clear, even in this rough rendering.

I begin at the crown of his head, which is lousy, filthy,
  Dark-skinned, scabbed, foul at the back,
Where nits are congregated in swarms
  In his withered, tossed, shock hair.

There are hundreds of wrinkles close together on his twisted shaggy forehead,
  Which looks like a miserable cat in a back yard,
And his swollen eyebrows like thickets of twisted blackthorn
  With batches of speckled lice hidden in them.

The clown's eyebrows are like plough-handles
  As they crookedly overhang his sunken eyes,
And ass's ears, like muck shovels,
  Coming fully down to his rough shoulders.

There is much rheum, a soft mass of matter,
  A greasy overflow and a fresh secretion,
About the crooked eyes of the thieving clown,
  The wooden dunce who is not worth a straw.

The hollows of his round eyes would be fitting receptacles
  For a cuckoo in danger of hatching to nest in,
His cheek bluish, very pale, miserably-speckled, grey, bare,
  Much wrinkled, bent, sallow-complexioned.

Through the holes of his nostrils may indeed be seen
  His copper-coloured palate and indeed his windpipe,
In which at a feast, running, he would swallow rubbish,
  Which imparts a damp, putrid smell to his vomit.

A long unkempt thing is his milt tongue
  Stretched bent across the back of his mouth.
And his sticks of yellow-flanged wormy teeth
  Would tear hungrily the back of a crust.

There is, on his rough windpipe, a mass of scabs
  And a large spot of yellow matter beneath them.

The villain's chest is like a carrion log
  Being rent asunder by dogs in a black cess-pool.

The foul deaf fellow has a narrow crooked shoulder
  And a dun-coloured hip very slight,
With thousands of blue veins weakly crossing each other
  Along the expanse of his foul brutish stomach.

[At this point Father Dinneen seems to have gelded the text.]

A miserable, speckled shin, gnarled,
  Burnt, with thick and bent hair;
Crooked heels, foppish gait,
  And rough, heavy, big hoof feet.

Hands, soft, foul-smelling, deep-hollowed, cold, sharp,
  Sore, fresh-scarred, and with large palms;
And scabby, horny, angular, sharp-jointed
  Appear his hard, crooked, bent fingers.

DONAL MACCARTHY (c.1700)
Trans. REV. PATRICK DINNEEN

Last Lines

Looked on with disfavour by the English, who rightly suspected them of being Jacobite, and without the support of their traditional patrons, poets in 17th- and 18th-century Ireland knew great hardship. In these verses Egan O'Rahilly bewails his own fate as well as that of the 'princes of Munster' and the Stuart Pretender, who was in exile on the Continent.

I shall not call for help until they coffin me,
What good for me to call when hope of help is gone?
Princes of Munster that would have heard my cry
Will not rise from the dead because I am alone.

Mind shudders like a wave in this tempestuous mood,
My bowels and my heart are pierced and filled with pain
To see our lands, our hills, our gentle neighbourhood
A plot where any English upstart stakes his claim.

The Shannon and the Liffey and the tuneful Lee,
The Boyne and the Blackwater a sad music sing,
The waters of the west run red into the sea –
No matter what be trumps their knave will beat our king.

And I have never ceased weeping these useless tears,
I am a man, oppressed, afflicted, and undone,
Who where he wanders mourning no companion hears
Only some waterfall that has no cause to mourn.

Now I shall cease, death comes and I must not delay
By Laune and Lane and Lee diminished of their pride,
I shall go after the heroes, ay, into the clay,
My fathers followed theirs before Christ was crucified.

EGAN O' RAHILLY (c.1675–1729)
Trans. FRANK O'CONNOR

On the Death of Dawson

Colonel James Dawson of Ballynacoorty in the Glen of
Aherlow seems to have been a particularly unpleasant
example of the new ruling class. When he died in 1732,
John Clarach MacDonnell gave vent to his loathing in this
famous curse.

> Beneath these stones grey Dawson lies.
> A churlish blackguard gorged with blood;
> He loved to hear his victims' cries:
> May he now rot in Irish mud.

His table groaned beneath the weight
Of salmon, game and claret red;
Yet as he dined from costly plate,
Poor children starved for want of bread.

To Lazarus he closed his door,
Lest pity move him to the good;
The back he'd flog till shredded raw
Of any man who begged for wood.

While paupers froze through lack of fuel,
Whole forests in his hearth did burn;
Let him now blaze, as he was cruel
To others; let him suffering learn.

Unceasingly he broke the laws
Of God's true Church, the shameless dog;
Evicted by his bestial paws,
The people slept on moor or bog.

Contempt for others was his goad,
The needs of babes he'd basely spurn;
Cocytus henceforth's his abode,
Where scorching thirst and fires burn.

'Tis right that men like him should hang,
And John his son, the ne'er-do-well;
May dogs devour with hungry fang
His body as it lies in hell.

Breadwinners hanged, by his decree,
If twopence lacked from rent or tithes;
The table's turned, for now it's he
Who suffers torment, winces, writhes.

On him who stole the widow's mite
Let maggots feast until they spew;
A bonfire then let Satan light
And boil his bones as Irish stew.

Press hard, good stone, crush every vein,
His head, his eyes, his great black arse;
Let none of those who knew him deign
To pray for him at Holy Mass.

JOHN CLARACH MACDONNELL (1691–1754)
Trans. FRANK MURPHY

Dear Friend, Dear James

A poet must eat – and drink – whether he has patrons or not.
Forced to earn his living as a labourer, Owen Roe O'Sullivan pre-
pares to leave for Galway, where the pay for a day's work was
breakfast and a *real* (sixpence).
(To James Fitzgerald, asking him to put a handle on a spade)

Dear friend, dear James, your forebears made
The Geralds outshine lesser breeds.
With loving hands, to suit my spade,
Make me a handle fit for deeds.

With shouldered tool I'll need no goad,
I'm off to earn the workman's meal;
To Galway lies adventure's road,
Your spade will dig my daily real.

As daylight ebbs, so may my force,
The cursing steward won't be coy;
But I shall speak about the horse
In which Greek princes entered Troy.

Of Samson's mighty deeds I'll tell,
Of Alexander's lust for gore,

Of Caesar's rule, and all who fell
Before Achilles' sword in war.

Of slaughtered Fenians, of their plight,
Of Deirdre's beauty much I'll say;
My songs will coax the dimming light –
That's how, dear James, I'll pass the day.

As night comes down, with hempen cord
Inside my shirt my pay I'll tie;
Then saunter homeward like a lord
Who never spends, but you know why.

For we'll be thirsty, we'll not fail
The taverner at end of day.
In draughts of whiskey, pints of ale,
Together we shall spend my pay.

OWEN ROE O'SULLIVAN (1748–1784)
Trans. FRANK MURPHY

Remembrance of Things Past

Although the 'old families' found themselves swept aside, the
memory of what they had been lingered for a long time.

The Old Families

All the poor people (of Annesgrove, Co. Cork) are Roman
Catholics, and among them are the descendants of the old families
who once possessed the country, of which they still possess the
memory, insomuch, that a gentleman's labourer will regularly leave
to his son, by will, his master's estate . . .

At Clonells (Co. Roscommon), near Castlerea, lives O'Connor,
the direct descendant of Roderick O'Connor, who was king of
Connaught 6 or 700 years ago; there is a monument of him in
Roscommon church, with his scepter, &c. I was told as a certainty,
that this family were here long before the coming of the Milesians.

The possessions formerly so great are reduced to 3 or £400 a year, the family having fared in the revolutions of so many ages, much worse than the O'Niels and O'Briens. The common people pay him the greatest respect, and send him presents of cattle, &c. upon various occasions. They consider him as the Prince of a people involved in one common ruin.

Another great family in Connaught is Macdermot, who calls himself Prince of Coolavin; he lives at Collavin (Co. Sligo) and, though he has not above £100 a year, will not admit his children to sit down in his presence . . .

ARTHUR YOUNG, *A Tour of Ireland*, 1776–79

Burke's Domain

In the first half of the 19th century, when the language he wielded so well was in its death throes, a blind bard named Anthony Raftery roamed the West of Ireland. He described himself in one of his poems, which Frank O'Connor has translated, in these words:

> I am Raftery the poet,
> Full of hope and love,
> With eyes without light
> And calm without torment.
>
> Going west on my journey
> By the light of my heart,
> Weak and tired
> To my road's end.
>
> Look at me now,
> My face to the wall,
> Playing music
> To empty pockets.

Soon the Famine would overwhelm what remained of Gaeldom among the peasants. Raftery, who shared their destitution – their 'empty pockets' – composed poems which took such a hold on his unlettered listeners that often they could still recite them from memory many years later. One of his patrons was Patrick Burke, of

Ballinahevna near Craughwell in Co. Galway. Raftery honoured and immortalised him with this simple song which expresses – to paraphrase Charles de Gaulle – *une certaine idée de l'Irlande.*

I know a house of welcome, where all may step inside:
To pauper as to rich man, its door is open wide.
I've searched throughout the kingdom, but nowhere did I find
Another host as generous, another half as kind.
At midnight you might come here, and still you'd hear the throng,
The voices raised in laughter, in poetry and song.
For who would think of sleeping while yet there's wine to drink?
And how could I not praise him as long as I have ink?

For Burke is friend to Nugent, to Daly's ancient line;
The Frenches call to sup here, the Blakes are proud to dine.
No Browne, no man of fortune, no gentleman or heir
Would deem himself dishonoured to sample Patrick's fare.
God's priests here hold their station, the sinner they unbind,
And here, as did their fathers, men bring their corn to grind.
Above all other places that I might see or gain,
I know of none to equal patrician Burke's Domain.

Here fish swim in the river, and fruit profusely grows,
Both walnuts and red apples, bright cherries and black sloes.
Green foliage decks the treetops, whose heavy boughs hang down
With damsons far excelling those money buys in town.
From Hallowe'en to Christmas, the cuckoo's voice is heard,
While woodcock, thrush and blackbird, in turn each sings his word.
With shouts the valleys echo of hunters whom the dawn
Has roused to follow foxes, or hound the startled fawn.

Around lie woods and meadows, beneath the cloudless sky,
Which stretches over croplands of wheat and rape and rye.
Firm ears of oats and barley, in fields below the wold,
As if obeying Midas, turn slowly into gold.
In spring the ploughman labours, colossal horses toil,

Before the sower scatters his seed in fertile soil.
And mindful of his workmen made thirsty by their task,
Burke sends up from his cellar another oaken cask.

Indoors, the servants scurry, as dishes they prepare,
To lay on lordly tables with silver old and rare.
With negus or with whiskey, they fill decanters fine,
Then charge the crystal glasses with choicest Bordeaux wine.
And tankards they make ready, which every honoured guest
Will raise to toast his neighbour, to wish him fortune's best.
Then while some play backgammon, a harpist plucks the strings,
The company united in robust chorus sings.

The cooks, at work since sunrise, will have due cause to boast
Of all the geese and ducklings, the turkeys they will roast.
For dinner they'll serve mutton, and legs of tender ham,
Good beef in joints and barons, and specially fattened lamb.
Fresh ling we'll have and mackeral, with lobster, crab and wrasse;
The turbot too will be there, the gurnet and the bass.
And noble though the pike is, arrayed upon a dish,
In splendour none can rival the salmon, prince of fish.

A man could travel Ireland from Cork to Donegal,
In search of one fair woman whose virtue conquers all.
Beyond the price of rubies, Burke's good and generous spouse
Outshines all other treasures inside her well-kept house.
From Lammas until Christmas, of alms she never tires.
But bread she gives to beggars, or turf for winter fires.
And if these lines outlast me, when I am laid to rest,
Content am I recording that she was Ireland's best.

The ewe her lambkin suckles, the mare brings forth her foal,
While sated new-born piglets beside their mother loll.
Here doe-eyed heifers dally, as sleepy herdsmen drowse
On grassland by the river, or milk complacent cows.

In Connaught, Leinster, Ulster, in Munster and in Meath,
The name *de Burgh* is honoured, which Normans did bequeath.
But great as were the glories his forebears did attain,
In bounty none surpasses the host of Burke's Domain.

ANTHONY RAFTERY (1784–1835)
Trans. FRANK MURPHY

DAILY LIFE

Fishermen hauling in salmon

As most people were illiterate, a great part of what we know about their daily life comes from accounts written by visitors to Ireland, or by people whose education set them apart from the common folk.

Market Day

Limerick

I passed through one of the narrow streets of the old town, in order to find out the house of a former tenant of mine, who kept a feather and skin shop in that part of the city. It was on market day, and the scene was equally remarkable for bustle and dinginess. The street, badly paved, and ancle deep in black mire, was covered with small wooden tables, extending nearly the whole length, on which were exposed for sale pig's pettitoes, ears, knees, tongues of beef, iron and brass nails, huge cakes of coarse griddle bread, heads of cabbage, scissors and smoothing irons, locks, onions, sickles, gingerbread, Saint Patrick's brogues, and other articles of humble luxury as well as use. Booths were hung with shawls and handkerchiefs, striped heavy woollen waistcoats, and beads of glass and horn. In one corner was an old woman herding a basket of withered apples, in another was a half-starved, ragged family, endeavouring to procure a few pence to pay for a night's lodging, by singing, in grand chorus a satirical effusion on the new ambition which had possessed the cottage belles, of figuring in 'drab mantles and cassimer shawls'. The space left between the booths and tables was crowded with country people, habited in various, and some in grotesque costumes. A woman was seen with her husband's new felt hat, thrust for the sake of convenience, down upon her own cap and ribbons. A man who had made a similar purchase, forebore to strip the article of the paper in which it was made up, and walked through the street unconscious of his comical appearance, and unheeded by those around him.

GERALD GRIFFIN, *Tracy's Ambition*, 1830

Cashel

The second day I spent at Cashel, was market day; and among other sights, I was greatly amused by the country people driving bargains for pigs. A man, a pig-dealer, would come to a countryman who held a pig by a string. 'How much do you ask?' – '28s.,' the answer might be. 'Hold out your hand,' says the buyer; and the proprietor of the pigs holds out his hand accordingly: the buyer places a penny in it, and then strikes it with a force that might break the back of an ox: 'Will ye take 20s.?' The other shakes his head – 'Ask 24s. and see if I'll give it ye,' says the pig-merchant. The owner again shakes his head. It is probable that by this time, some one among the bystan-

Galway market on a rainy day

ders – for there is always a circle formed round a bargain-making – endeavours to accommodate matters; for it is another instance of the kindly feeling towards each other, that all around are anxious that the bargain should be concluded. Again, the merchant says, 'Hold out your hand,' and again a tremendous blow is struck, and a new offer made, till at last they come within a shilling perhaps of each other's terms; when the bargain is struck; and the shilling about which they differed, and probably two or three others, are spent in whiskey punch 'screeching hot'.

HENRY D. INGLIS, *Journey Throughout Ireland*, 1834

Turf

The most common method of providing turf fuel in Ireland requires six distinct operations, viz. – cutting, spreading, footing, rickling, clamping and drawing home.

Slane or turf spade

1. The first operation, or cutting, requires four men with two turf-barrows. The chief or strongest man is selected for the turf-spade (slane) and ... the second man in strength is put to the turf-barrows ... The third man goes before the turf-cutter, paving and levelling the banks, and a man lifts the turf two at a time ... and deposits them on the barrows. The four men employed at this work are usually paid about one shilling a day, a somewhat higher rate than for ordinary labour. The quantity cut and wheeled out by this party in one day is generally termed a dark, which, therefore, is an indefinite quantity, dependent upon the strength and industry of the workmen. Still, when a cottager speaks of his fuel, he estimates it at so many darks; and a year's supply for a cottage with one fire varies from two to four darks ... When each barrowful of turf is wheeled from the bank to its proper place in the 'spread-field', it is simply tumbled off, and left as it falls for about a week.

2. The second operation is the spreading or scattering the turf from the small barrow-heaps, so as completely to cover the 'spread-field', turning up the sides of the turf that were under-neath. This work is usually done by women and children. One woman can spread three darks in a day. The turf remains about a week thus spread out.

3. The third operation is footing, which means collecting the turf into parcels of about six each, placing them on end in a circle, and supported against each other by meeting in a point at the top. This is done by women and children. One woman can foot at the rate of a dark per day. The turf remains in the footings about ten days.

4. The fourth operation is rickling. A rickle contains about ten footings laid on their sides, one turf deep, and built up about two feet high. The rickling is done by women and children. Two women can rickle three darks in a day. The turf remains in rickles about fourteen days.

5. The fifth operation is clamping. The clamps are small stacks about twelve feet long, six feet high, and four feet wide; they are placed on the most convenient spots for the carts to approach. They remain in the clamps until it is convenient to bring them home ... A man can clamp a dark in a day and a half.

6. The sixth operation is drawing home, when the turf is usually built in a large stack exposed to the weather. Those who are careful and provident, either put them in sheds, or thatch their stacks over. It is very essential, when building the permanent stack, to place it in a proper aspect, presenting one end to the prevalent wind; and it should be built in what is termed 'leets', meaning that it should have a number of well-built transverse sections, so formed that a month's or a fortnight's supply may be put into the house from the

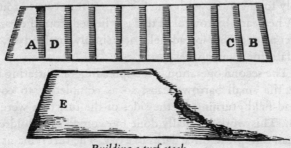

Building a turf-stack

sheltered end at a time, leaving always a square face to the stack. Thus, in building, the stack should be commenced at the end, A, towards the storm, and a triangular leet, A, is built up. Afterwards the leet, D, is built up, &c. &c.; and when the stack is to be used, the leet, B, at the reverse end, should be the first taken in; the leet, C, the second, and so on. The outside or weather turf should, in building, be slightly inclined, so as to shed the drop out, as in B, C, &c., not inclined in or level, as shown in E. In short, every possible scheme should be used to preserve the turf from wet . . .

MRS S. C. HALL, *Ireland,* 1841

Transport

The Irish 'Carr'

There are no Carts or Waggons here, they have Carrs, which are a kind of Sledge, set on two solid wooden Wheels strok'd with Iron, and drawn by a single horse; they carry great Burthens, some 600 Weight. They differ from the Welsh Carriages only in this, as *They* have no Wheels. These Carriages are undoubtedly the Best for preserving the Road.

JOHN LOVEDAY, *Diary of a Tour,* 1732

Traditional Irish car

A Bianconi car

A Trip to Dublin

Charles Bianconi, who was born in Lombardy in 1786, travelled around Ireland early in the 18th century selling cheap prints. Noticing how difficult is was to find transport, especially between small towns, he set up his own system of horse-drawn cars, which linked up with the mail coaches and the canal services. By the 1840s, when they were soon to be replaced by railways, more than one hundred of his cars were on the roads.

31st August . . . I left Callan (Co. Kilkenny) in the evening by Bianconi's car and went to Kilkenny for 1/8d. Here I stayed till nine p.m., when I caught the Mail Coach. It was a mild evening with a northerly wind. At half past two in the morning a heavy fog came on which lasted for two hours. I arrived at Dublin at seven a.m.

1st September . . . After coming from Callan overnight I went to Duffy's and other places to purchase goods . . .

4th September . . . Came from Dublin to Kilkenny in eleven hours for six shillings and sixpence by the daycoach. I walked from Kilkenny to Callan taking my time. I was home with my little orphans by nine o'clock of a mild night.

HUMPHREY O'SULLIVAN, *Diary*, 1829
Trans. FRANK MURPHY

Travelling in the Rain

I had often anticipated, but I now had the full experience of, the misery of an Irish car in a storm; and I can, without hesitation, pronounce it to be the most wretched of all possible means of conveyance; I certainly was never exposed to such drenching rain. MacIntosh's cloak, and the waterproof boots, which I purchased last year at Tronyem, totally gave way to the merciless storm with which I was so piteously pelted...

The wind was so violent, that we were several times obliged to take shelter under the lee of the cottages by the road-side, and once under that of a peat-stack... On entering one of the cottages to take shelter, at times when the wind and rain was so bad at to render it difficult to get the poor animal onwards, the general remark was, 'Dear, dear, what a day to be out in!'

JOHN BARROW, *A Tour Round Ireland,* 1835

The Peasant's Cabin

Late 17th Century

In the better sort of cabins there is generally one flock bed, seldom more, feathers being too costly; this serves the man and his wife, the rest all lie on straw, some with one sheet and blanket, others only their clothes and blanket to cover them. The cabins have seldom any floor but the earth, or rarely so much as a loft, some have windows, others none. They say it is of late years that chimneys are used, yet the house is never free from smoke. That they have no locks to their door is not because there are not thieves but because there is nothing to steal.

JOHN STEVENS, *Journal,* 1689–91

First Half of the 19th Century

The Donovans' house was of the humblest description. The floor of it was about sixteen feet by twelve; its furniture rude and scanty. To

Peasant's cabin

the right of the fire was a bed, the four posts of which ran up to the low roof; it was curtained with straw mats, with the exception of an opening about a foot and a half wide on the side next the fire, through which those who slept in it passed. A little below the foot of the bed were ranged a few shelves of deal, supported by pins of wood driven into the wall. These constituted the dresser. In the lower end of the house stood a potato-bin, made up of stakes driven into the floor, and wrought with strong wicker-work. Tied to another stake beside this bin stood a cow, whose hinder part projected so close to the door, that those who entered the cabin were compelled to push her over out of their way. This, indeed, was effected without much difficulty, for the animal became so habituated to the necessity of moving aside, that it was only necessary to lay the hand upon her. Above the door in the inside, almost touching the roof, was the hen-roost, made also of wicker-work; and opposite the bed, on the other side of the fire, stood a meal chest, its lid on a level with the little pane of glass which served as a window. An old straw chair, a few stools, a couple of pots, some wooden vessels and crockery, completed the furniture of the house. The pig . . . was not kept within the cabin, that filthy custom being now less common than formerly.

This catalogue of cottage furniture may appear . . . very miserable . . . However, if every cabin in Ireland were equally comfortable, the country would be comparatively happy.

WILLIAM CARLETON, *Traits and Stories of the Irish Peasantry*, 1830–33

Clothing
Brogues

Very little clothing serves them, and as for shoes and stockings much less. They wear brogues being quite plain without so much as one lift of a heel, and all are sowed with thongs, and the leather not curried, so that in wearing it grows hard as a board, and therefore many always keep them wet, but the wiser that can afford it grease them often and that makes them supple.

JOHN STEVENS, *Journal*, 1689–91

The Irish Woman

See crowds of females, and many of them otherwise well drest, flocking barefooted (*more Cambrico*) to the fair, and near the town a large group performing ablutions in a pond, preparatory to putting on their stockings . . .

To the female peasant, I would recommend the adoption of the black beaver hat, which is universally worn in Wales, and gives a look of comfort and neatness; whereas the want of covering to the head, and the cap loosely flying in the wind, with the long flowing hair, give the sex the appearance of maniacs.

SIR RICHARD COLT HOARE, *Journal of a Tour in Ireland*, 1806

Colours and Cloaks

In the county Limerick, the men's dress is invariably of a grey (or pepper and salt colour) produced by a mixture of black and white wool without any process of dying. In the eastern parts of the county Cork, dark blue is the predominant colour; whilst, in the western parts and in the county Kerry, light or powder blue is almost universally worn. The same peculiarity, but in a less degree, extends to female dress. In the eastern baronies of the county Cork and county Limerick, cloaks of the brightest red are seen. Previous to the rebellion of 1798, the former colour was more commonly worn than it has been since, and about that time red became generally disused. A contemptuous expression of the English soldiers at that time, after any contest, was 'now a woman seen at a distance in her scarlet cloak would strike a panic throughout the whole country'.

The cloak is a part of dress apparently never superfluous to an Irish woman, and is constantly used with the hood over the head, even during the hottest days of summer; those who are not so fortunate as to possess a cloak turn the skirt of their gown or an apron over their shoulders, and in this *huddled* style proceed about their outdoor occupations with as little alacrity as might be expected. A brown stuff gown and green petticoat is the popular costume, with stockings of the brightest blue, but these latter are by no means an indispensable part of dress, and, truth to say, are not often seen; neither are shoes considered of any importance, but rather a fatiguing incumbrance, gladly dismissed when opportunity offers, and scarcely ever worn but on the Sabbath and other holidays. Journies are invariably performed barefooted, the shoes and stockings tied together and thrown across the arm.

'A female in the lower ranks of life cares but little for the other portions of her dress if she has a good cloak . . .'

There is, however, a strong desire to possess a pair of silver buckles or a silver clasp for the cloak, such ornaments being considered as marks of consequence, and they are handed down from mother to daughter with the greatest care. Bonnets are quite unknown, the hood of the cloak answering all demands for the head, which is, however, sometimes adorned by a high cauled mob cap. The fodaheen, or little hood, is also a favourite head-dress, more particularly with those advanced in life, and is formed by a handkerchief carefully folded round the head and tied in a knot under the chin.

T. CROFTON CROKER, *Researches in the South of Ireland*, 1824

Kerryman

Connemara

The men wear a sort of warm, grey frieze cloth for clothing and blankets; the women have it dyed red, for their cloaks and petti-coats, which is almost the universal colour in Connemara. Their usual dress is a red jacket and red petticoat, without stockings or shoes.

JOHN BARROW, *A Tour Round Ireland*, 1835

Food

La Cuisine Irlandaise

They eat here, as well as in some parts of Scotland, cakes called kets, which they bake on thin iron plates over a fire; being sufficiently baked on one side, they turn them on the other, till they become as dry as a biscuit. They are made without leaven, and sometimes so ill baked that a person who is not used to them cannot eat them; nevertheless throughout all the inns on the road no other sort of bread is eaten; however, they do not spare to cover them with butter, and thick cheese, here very cheap, costing only a penny a pound. The common people live chiefly on this, especially in places distant from the rivers and lakes . . .

This kingdom . . . is the richest of all Europe in things necessary for human life, but the poorest in money. This causes provisions to be so cheap, that butter and cheese are commonly sold at a penny the pound; a pound of beef, at the butchery, for eight deniers; veal and mutton a penny; a large salmon just out of the sea, threepence; a large fresh cod, twopence; a pair of soles, or quaviver, above a foot broad, a penny; an hundred herrings, threepence; so that one is served with flesh and fish in the best manner for twelvepence a day. In fine, this is the land of plenty. And, moreover, on the road, if you drink two pennyworth of beer at a public-house, they will give you of bread, meat, butter, cheese, fish, as much as you choose; and for all this you only pay your twopence for the beer, it being the custom of the kingdom, as I have experienced wherever I have been . . .

At Dromore I [ate] of a salad made according to the mode of the country, of I know not what herbs; I think there were sorrel and beets chopt together; it represented the form of a fish, the whole without oil or salt, and only a little vinegar made of beer, and a quantity of sugar strewed over it, that it resembled Mount Etna covered with snow, so that it is impossible to be eaten by any one not accustomed to it. I made my host laugh heartily in the presence of a gentleman, a lord of the town, on asking for oil to season this salad, according to the French fashion, and after having dressed it, I persuaded the gentleman to taste it, who was pleased to hear me speak of the state and customs of France ...

ALBERT JOUVIN DE ROCHEFORT, *Ireland under the Restoration*, 1667

A Catalogue

[The diet of the people comprises] Usquebath [whiskey], Oatcakes, Sweet milk [skimmed milk], Bonny clobber [sour buttermilk], Mallahaune [cheese], Dilisk [dulse, a kind of seaweed], Slugane [sloak, also a kind of seaweed], good Spoals [joints of meat].

THOMAS DINELEY, *Journal*, 17th century

The Common Fare

The people generally [are] the greatest lovers of milk I ever saw, which they eat and drink above twenty several sorts of ways, and what is strangest for the most part love it best when sourest. They keep it in sour vessels and from time to time till it grows thick,

Stool, piggin (pail) for buttermilk, and borrane

and sometimes to that perfection it will perfume a whole house, but generally speaking they order it so that it is impossible to boil it without curdling four days after it comes from the cow. Oaten and barley bread is the common fare, and that in cakes, and ground by hand. None but the best sort or the inhabitants of great towns eat wheat, or bread baked in an oven, or ground in a mill. The meaner people content themselves with little bread but instead thereof eat potatoes, which with sour milk is the chief part of their diet, their drink for the most part water, sometimes coloured with milk; beer or ale they seldom taste unless they sell something considerable in a market town.

JOHN STEVENS, *Journal,* 1689–91

Plain Dishes

The second class of Irish gentry still retain the ancient mode of eating their food. They have little else than plain dishes, as they are termed – that is, great joints of meat, ribs and sirloins, shoulders and legs, which retaining their ancient forms, instantly remind us of the animal to which they belonged.

J. GAMBLE, *A View of Society and Manners in the North of Ireland,* 1812

A Draper's Diary

Schoolmaster and draper in the town of Callan, Co. Kilkenny, Humphrey O'Sullivan (1780-1838) kept a diary which tells much about the ordinary life of his day. On 30th July 1830, for example, he wrote:

This is what we eat, my family and me: we have a hot meal, oatmeal porridge with milk in the morning, then wheaten bread and milk at one o'clock. This midday meal is a cold one. Then potatoes and meat or butter in the evening.

Modest as it was, this dull diet nonetheless indicated a better standard of living than that of many of his countrymen. These entries from the year 1828 suggest that the best table in Callan was to be found at the house of the parish priest.

20th February Ash Wednesday . . . Had bread and porridge for dinner . . .

21st February Had coiblide for dinner. It is incorrect to call it colcannon, as it has neither kale nor cauliflower nor white cabbage in it; but potatoes, new whole milk, good salted butter, and salt; pepper to warm me and onion . . . And me and the children and my poor loving wife eating our fill without want or excess . . .

6th April Easter Sunday . . . Had smoked bacon and chicken for dinner . . .

27th May I recall the time, around 35 years ago, when every able-bodied farmer had peas and beans, but they're outdated now because of potatoes, and few sow them except the well-born . . .

20th June Had dinner with Father James Hannebery. We ate two fine fat sweet trout, one of them as large as a small salmon, We ate hard-boiled hens' eggs, and asparagus dipped in butter, new milk and salt. We had port and scailtin as good as any I've ever had, and, of course, we weren't going to waste it!

18th July . . . Seven of us had dinner at the Rose Tavern. We had salmon and fresh hake and new potatoes, bread, ale and scailtin. This cost us three shillings each . . .

22nd July . . . Had dinner with the parish priest, Father James Hannebery. We ate boiled leg of mutton and roast fowl with spicy stuffing. We drank scailtin and tea, and sang Irish songs till ten o'clock.

14th September . . . Four of us had dinner with Father James Hannebery. We ate boiled leg of mutton with parsnips and turnips, roast goose with green peas and stuffing, we had a dish of tripes cooked in new milk, we drank port, scailtin and tea, and sang Irish songs and on we went till eleven o'clock jovial, jocular, joyful and jolly.

28th September . . . I spent the evening and part of the night at the house of the parish priest, Father James Hannebery. We had three dishes, ox-tripe cooked in butter and new milk, bacon with kidney and cauliflower, roast duck with green peas. We drank scailtín and sang till ten o'clock . . .

5th October . . . From four o'clock on, a sunny day with no cloud. We had an excellent dinner at the house of the parish priest. There were seven men there and one young woman. We had leg of mutton, bacon, chicken and white cabbage, and two roast ducks with green peas. We drank white wine and port and scailtin a-plenty till eleven o'clock.

HUMPHREY O'SULLIVAN, *Diary*, 1828
Trans. FRANK MURPHY

An Irish Feast

An excellent dinner, plain and abundant, was spread out upon the table. It consisted of the usual materials which constitute an Irish feast in the house of a wealthy farmer, whose pride is to compel every guest to eat so long as he can swallow a morsel. There were geese and fowl of all kinds – shoulders of mutton, laughing-potatoes, carrots, parsnips, and cabbage, together with an immense pudding, boiled in a clean sheet, and ingeniously kept together with long straws drawn through it in all directions . . . When Father Finnerty had given a short grace . . . the operations of the table . . . commenced.

WILLIAM CARLETON, *Traits and Stories of the Irish Peasantry*, 1830–33

Workhouse Diet

The dietary in most common use consists of a daily allowance of – for breakfast, to adults, 7 ounces of oatmeal made into 'stirabout', one pint of buttermilk, or half a pint of new milk; for dinner – 3½ pounds of potatoes, and 1 quart of buttermilk; children, 5 to 14, 3½ ounces of oatmeal for breakfast; dinner, 2 pounds of potatoes; supper, 6 ounces of bread, and 1 pint of new milk, daily. Infants, the sick, infirm, &c., dieted as directed by medical officer. Two meals a day only are allowed; except in

Women at Killarney market

some districts, 'where the bulk of the labouring population can
and do usually provide for themselves three meals'. Children
have three meals. Meat is not given; it is unnecessary to say that
meat is a 'luxury' rarely tasted by the Irish peasant out of the
workhouse. In Dublin, Cork, and other localities, however, soup
and other descriptions of food are given to the paupers; in Dublin
we saw them dining upon rice, which they at first loudly pro-
tested against, but to which they afterwards became accustomed.
Potatoes were then at a very high price.

MRS S. C. HALL, *Ireland*, 1841

Cream Cheese

The gardener . . . showed me the Irish manner of making a kind of cream cheese. This is done by putting the thick sour cream into a cloth, hanging it up till the thinner part has dropped from it, and then putting it into a hoop, like a sieve, and pressing it down tightly.

A. NICHOLSON, *The Bible in Ireland*, 1844–45

Spoileen

In a great portion of Ireland there are to be found in all fairs, what the people term *spoileen* tents – that is, tents in which fresh mutton is boiled, and sold out, with bread and soup, to all customers. I know not how it happens; but be the motive, or cause, what it may, scarcely any one ever goes into a spoileen tent, unless in a mood of mirth and jocularity. To eat spoileen seriously, would be as rare a sight as to witness a wife dancing on her husband's coffin. It is very difficult, indeed, to ascertain the reason why the eating of fresh mutton, in such circumstances, is always associated with a spirit of strong ridicule and humour. At all events, nothing can exceed the mirth that is always to be found among the parties who frequent such tents. Fun, laughter, jest, banter, attack, and repartee fly about in all directions, and the only sounds heard are those of light-hearted noise and enjoyment.

Perhaps, if the cause of this were closely traced, it might be found to consist in a sense of shame, which Paddy good-humouredly attempts to laugh away. It is well known that the great body of the people pass through life without ever tasting beef or mutton – a circumstance which every one acquainted with the country knows to be true. It is also a fact, that nineteen out of every twenty who go in to eat spoileen, are actuated more by curiosity than hunger, inasmuch as they consist of such persons as have never tasted it before. This, therefore, being generally known, and each possessing a latent consciousness of its truth, it is considered best to take the matter in good humour, and escape the shame of the thing, together with the poverty it implies, by turning it into ridicule and jest. This, indeed, is pretty evident, from the nature of the spoileen-keeper's observations on being paid, which are usually, 'Thank you, Barney, you may now considher yourself a gintleman;' or, if a female, 'Long life to you, Bridget; you may now go into high life any time . . .'

The spoileen tents, in general, are pretty large, sometimes one, occasionally two fires being kept in each. Over these, placed upon three large stones, or suspended from three poles, united at top, is the pot or pots in which the spoileen is boiled; whilst patiently, in a corner of the tent, stand the poor invalid sheep that are doomed, as necessity may require, to furnish forth this humorous entertainment. It is called *spoileen*, because the feast usually consists of *spoiled* mutton – that is, mutton that could not otherwise be sold as sound.

[Spoiled though the mutton may have been, this explanation of the word's origin is incorrect. The correct etymology is given in the glossary at the end of the book.]

WILLIAM CARLETON, *Valentine McClutchy*, 1845

Thanksgiving after Meals

We give thanks for this food to the great God of all the powers on account of his gift to us. May the great God of all the powers defend us against our enemies of mind and body. If it is well we are now in the grace of God, and the world, may we be seven times better a year hence, and if not better, not worse.

Apparently traditional, from *St. Patrick's Prayer Book*, c.1900

Smoking

The Family Pipe

They all smoke, women as well as men, and a pipe an inch long serves the whole family several years and though never so black or foul is never suffered to be burnt. Seven or eight will gather to the smoking of a pipe and each taking two or three whiffs gives it to his neighbour, commonly holding his mouth full of smoke till the pipe comes about to him again. They are also much given to taking of snuff.

JOHN STEVENS, *Journal*, 1689–91

Pipe-smokers

The Little Brown Mallett

According to the translator of this popular little song, the name *Smachteen Cron* was applied to 'a stout description of tobacco, smuggled into Ireland . . . and in which an extensive trade was carried on in Munster'.

> Arise! get up my girl!
> Boil potatoes and meat!
> Here comes up the garden
> The lad with the *Smachteen Cron*!
>
> Oro, ro, my *Smachteen*!
> Love of my soul, my *Smachteen*!
> Oro, ro, my *Smachteen*!
> O my *Smachteen Cron*!

Anon. c.1750
Trans. JAMES CLARENCE MANGAN

Whiskey

Sassenachs, Beware!

Let all English be recommended to be very careful of whiskey, which experience teaches to be a very deleterious drink. Natives say that it is wholesome, and may be sometimes seen to use it with impunity; but the whiskey-fever is naturally more fatal to strangers than inhabitants of the country; and whereas an Irishman will sometimes imbibe a half-dozen tumblers of the posion, two glasses will be often found to cause headaches, heartburns, and fevers to a person newly arrived in the country. The said whiskey is always to be had for the asking, but is not produced at the bettermost sort of tables.

WILLIAM MAKEPEACE THACKERAY, *Irish Sketch Book*, 1843

O'Tuomy's Drinking Song

O'Tuomy's tavern in Mungret Street, Limerick, was a popular meeting place for poets in the 18th century. This drinking song was written by the innkeeper, a poet himself, who presided over the assemblies of poets which in the 18th century took the place of the old bardic schools.

I sell the best brandy and sherry,
To make my good customers merry;
  But, at times their finances
  Run short, as it chances,
And then I feel very sad, very!

Here's brandy! Come, fill up your tumbler,
Or ale, if your liking be humbler,
  And, while you've a shilling,
  Keep filling and swilling,
A fig for the growls of the grumbler!

I like, when I'm quite at my leisure,
Mirth, music, and all sorts of pleasure.
  When Margery's bringing
  The glass, I like singing
With bards – if they drink within measure.

Libation I pour on libation,
I sing the past fame of our nation
  For valour-won glory,
  For song and for story,
This, this is my grand recreation!

JOHN O'TUOMY (1708–1775)
Trans. JAMES CLARENCE MANGAN

Andrew McGrath's Reply to John O'Tuomy

O, Tuomy! you boast yourself handy
At selling good ale and bright brandy,
  But the fact is your liquor
  Makes every one sicker,
I tell you that, I, your friend Andy.

Again, you affect to be witty,
And your customers – more is the pity –
  Give in to your folly,
  While you, when you're jolly,
Troll forth some ridiculous ditty.

But your poems and pints, by your favour,
Are alike wholly wanting in flavour,
  Because it's your pleasure,
  You give us short measure,
And your ale has a ditch-water savour!

Vile swash do you sell us for porter,
And you draw the cask shorter and shorter;
  Your guests, then, disdaining
  To think of complaining,
Go tipple in some other quarter.

Very oft in your scant overfrothing
Tin quarts we found little or nothing;
  They could very ill follow
  The road, who would swallow
Such stuff for the inner man's clothing!

You sit gaily enough at the table,
But in spite of your mirth you are able
  To chalk down each tankard,
  And if a man drank hard
On tick – oh! we'd have such a Babel!

You bow to the floor's very level,
When customers enter to revel,
  But if one in shy raiment
  Takes drink without payment,
You score it against the poor devil.

When quitting your house rather heady,
They'll get nought without more of 'the ready'.
  You leave them to stumble
  And stagger and tumble
Into dykes, as folk will when unsteady.

Two vintners late went about killing
Men's fame by their vile Jack-and-Gilling;
  Now, Tuomy, I tell you
  I know very well you
Would, too, sell us all for a shilling.

The Old Bards never vainly shall woo me,
But your tricks and your capers, O'Tuomy,
  Have nought in them winning –
  You jest and keep grinning,
But your thoughts are all guileful and gloomy!

ANDREW McGRATH (c.1707–1795)
Trans. JAMES CLARENCE MANGAN

Wooden drinking vessels

THE STRUGGLE TO SURVIVE

Beggars accosting travellers in Cork

For most people throughout this period, living as they did in very harsh circumstances, the chief concern was survival. Would the lightning strike their thatched roof? Would the harvest be a good one? Would they be able to pay the rent, and keep their few stony acres? Would some of their children, at least, live to be adult, and keep them in their old age?

Winter

5th February Bitter grey frosty morning. At one o'clock snow began falling in small, hard flakes, with the cold wind coming in from the southeast. It is the coldest day I have known so far this year... Snowflakes as small as particles of sand, as hard as grain, as dry as oatmeal, driven by the cold wind all through the day until nightfall. It is a distressing night for anyone travelling south-east. No matter how well-sealed the house, this bitter wind finds a crack somewhere to drive the ever-falling snow inside. May God have pity on those in houses where there is no fire.

HUMPHREY O'SULLIVAN, *Diary*, 1830
Trans. FRANK MURPHY

The Seven Days of the Week

A prayer acknowledging man's dependance on God.

O God, who created heaven and earth,
Sun and moon, and divided the waters,
Keep not in mind the burden of our sins,
But share my hardship, and on Sunday answer me.

O Healer who tends me, and One True Lamb,
Who came from heaven to keep me from the fiery pit,
Vex me not in want or lasting need,
But share my hardship, and on Monday dispel my sorrow.

O Holy Spirit proceeding from the Father and the Mighty Son,
Who fills my soul with light and the fullness of grace,
Be not at enmity with us,
But undo my hardship, and on Tuesday dispel my fatigue.

O Blessèd Trinity, three dwelling as one,
All equal in sovereign power,
Dispel from me my tedious dire grief,
And all illness, and on Wednesday answer me.

O Christ, I beseech Thee, Nurse of gentle mien,
Who suffered hardship to buy our fair salvation,
Worn through illness and want am I, weak and empty;
Dispel my fatigue, and on Thursday answer me.

No meat have I, no horse, no endowment of cattle,
No wealth, no strength, no treasure, no sustenance;
Come to my aid without delay, or death will overtake me –
O Christ, take pity on me! on Friday answer me.

Wasting and fear rack my mind,
They kill my mind, and me a sobbing shape;
My need, my hardship, my illness, my bitter suffering,
Wash them from me: the week is done.

JOHN CLARACH MACDONNELL (1691–1754)
Trans. FRANK MURPHY

In the Sweat of his Brow

Clan Thomas

Although most people depended directly on the land for their living, we seldom see them at work there in Irish writing of the 17th and 18th centuries. This is because those who toiled in the fields or tended the herds were generally illiterate; the few who could write rarely deigned to describe the labouring masses. The following text, more a confirmation of this rule than an exception to it, is taken from a satire called *The Parliament of Clan Thomas.* Despite its irony, the text gives a rare glimpse of the common people in their element.

And Clan Thomas assembled full of vigour and pride from every place in which they were, as many of them as were bold in displaying action and force, until they all came to the Plain of Cashel . . .

When the time for reaping arrived, they came to one place, having with them their weapons of battle and strife; that is, their thick-wattled flails of tough wood and their keen-edged, fine-toothed reaping-hooks, and their rough-grained, side-smeared, wide-heeled, thick-greased clogs, and pointed awls of true beauty at the girdle of each man of them. His own ridge was appointed for each of them . . . Then they began eagerly and with buzzing:

and these stout men made a greedy, very vigorous attack on the beautiful plain of fine wheat before them. Far away was heard the hissing and the murmur of the very keen reaping-hooks over-throwing and cutting the full handfuls throughout the fair-flowered plain on every side. Manifest, truly, to the onlookers at a distance from them was the struggle of their long-beaked, thick, and frequent teeth, through their boiling-up and rage of fury to gain ground and precedence of one another. Truly, the air was dark for a long distance from them, on account of the black clouds, of the belching, and the breath of the young men.

The Parliament of Clan Thomas, c.1650
Trans. REV. PATRICK DINNEEN and TADHE O'DONOGHUE

The Faction

The old Gaelic Ireland which we glimpse in *The Parliament of Clan Thomas* can also be seen in the next text, which was written almost two centuries later. In the countryside, it seems, the strong patriarchal loyalties of the Irish died hard.

We heard music . . . [and] in coming nearer, we saw a motley company of men and women, with spades and buckets, some on foot and some on cars, following the sound of fife, flute and drum; and upon enquiry we found it was 'the faction'.

The custom of the peasantry, in this part at least of the country (Co. Kilkenny), has been to assemble in hundreds and reap down a harvest, or dig a farmer's potatoes, taking their musicians with them, who play through the day to amuse the labourers, and escort them home at night. This they will never do but for those whom they respect, and the generous farmer who has fed and paid his labourers well is sure to meet with a return of this kind. Women will go out and bind sheaves, rake and toss hay, pick up potatoes, etc; and the ambition manifested to accomplish much, and to do it well, is often beyond that of a paid labourer.

A. NICHOLSON, *The Bible in Ireland*, 1844-45

Bleaching linen cloth

Poverty

Balancing the Books

Nothing threatened the survival of the Irish peasant more than his poverty, which took many forms and left a lasting impression on foreign visitors. Among the poorest of the poor was the cottar (or cottier), a peasant who rented land at rates fixed by public competition. His precarious position may be judged from these figures.

The common mode of labour is that of cottars, they have a cabbin and an acre for 30 shillings, and 30 shillings the grass of a cow, reckining with them at five-pence a day the year round; other labour vibrates from four-pence to six-pence. A cottar with a middling family will have two cows; there is not one without a cow. All of them keep as many pigs as they can rear, and some poultry. Their circumstances are rather better than 20 years ago.

A COTTAR'S EXPENSES

Rent of a cabin and an acre.	£1.10. 0.
Two cows.	3. 0. 0.
Hay for ditto, one ton.	1.15. 0.
Tythe.	0. 4. 0.
Hearth money.	0. 2. 0.
One stone of wool a year for the man, one for the woman, and two stones for three children; this is what they ought to have, but the fact does not exceed two stone, one at 17s. and one at 8s.	1. 5. 0.
Tools.	0. 5. 0.
Turf, whether bought or in their own labour.	1. 0. 0.
Flax seed, five or six pottles at 8d.	0. 3. 6.
Breaking and scutching, eight stone, at 10d.	0. 6. 8.
Heckling, ditto, at 10d.	0. 6. 8.
Weaving 336 bandles, at 1s.1d. a score.	0.16. 6.
N.B. After heckling 56lb. flax, the rest is tow, which they spin for bags, etc.	
Two pair of brogues, 9s.9d., and 4 pair soles, 1s.10d. each, 7s.4d.	0.17. 1.
A pair of woman's shoes, 3s.3d., and a pair of soles, 1s.5d.	0. 4. 8.
A boy of fourteen, two pair, at 2s.2d., soles, 1s.1d.	0. 3. 3.
A hat, 2s.8d., the boy one, 1s.6d.	0. 4. 2.
	£12. 3. 6.

HIS RECEIPT

Deduct from		365 days
Sundays	52	
Holyday	1	
Bad weather	10	
Own work	48	
	111	

Remain at 5d.	254	5. 5.10.
The boy of twelve or fourteen, 3½d. a day		3.14. 1.
Two pigs, one cat, the other sold for		15. 0.
Two calves, one 20s. one 10s		1.10. 0.
		£11. 4.11.

N.B. Chickens and ducks pay for salt, soap, and candles, and they eat the geese.

When my informant, who was a poor man, had finished, I demanded how the 20s. deficiency, with whiskey, and the priest, were to be paid; the answer was, that *he must not eat his geese and pig, or else not dress so well,* which probably is the case. Their acre of garden feeds them the year through; nine months on potatoes, and the other three on oaten bread, from their own oats. The consumption of potatoes [has] not increased in twenty years. A family of five persons will eat and waste forty-two stone of potatoes in a week.

ARTHUR YOUNG, *A Tour in Ireland,* 1776–79

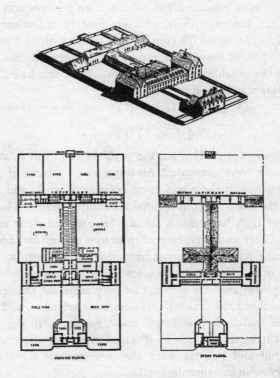

Model workhouse (first half of the 19th century)

Pigs

The cabins I found wretched in the extreme – many *without even a pig in them*. This, I put in italics; for a new light had now begun to dawn upon me. I used to be shocked at seeing a pig's snout at a cabin door, and looked upon such a spectacle as a proof of wretchedness; but I now began to bless the sight, and to pity more, the poor wretches who possessed no pig. It is true, indeed, that things were still better when a pig-stye was visible; for that gave evidence both of the existence of the pig, and of the superior comfort of its owner: but still, it was always to me a pleasant sight, where, if no pig-stye was visible, I saw him that pays the 'rint' walk leisurely in and out of the cabin door, or heard his comfortable grunt within. The greatest example of individual prosperity I observed among the poor in the neighbourhood of Thomastown, was finding three pigs resident in one cabin.

HENRY D. INGLIS, *Journey Throughout Ireland*, 1834

A Fire in Thurles

A fire broke out in Thurles, the night before I left it, and several houses were consumed. An immense concourse of persons was present; and there was more noise than work; and strange to tell, the town was unprovided with a fire engine. The lower orders of Irish have much feeling for each other. It is a rare thing to hear an angry, or contemptuous expression, addressed to any one who is poor: commiseration of the destitute condition of others, is largely mingled in their complaints of their own poverty; and it is a fact, that they are most exemplary in the care that they take of their destitute relatives, and in the sacrifices which they willingly make for them. In the crowds which thronged the streets of Thurles, during the conflagration, loud and general were the lamentations for the poor 'crathurs' who lost their little all.

HENRY D. INGLIS, *Journey Throughout Ireland*, 1834

Kerry Cows Know Sunday

In some places, Donegal and Kerry, to name two, when everything else had failed, they had the habit of bleeding the cattle
'which they had not the courage to steal', says a contemporary
account: mixing sorrel through it, they boiled the blood into a
broth, and 'Kerry cows know Sunday' became a proverb, for it
was to provide the Sunday dinner they had to suffer.

DANIEL CORKERY, *The Hidden Ireland: A Study of Gaelic Munster in the*
Eighteenth Century, 1925

The Idleness of the Irish

If the Irish were so poor, said many Englishmen throughout this
period, they should blame themselves. A German visitor of the
mid-19th century gives his point of view.

The matter is, after all, exceedingly simple, and most easy of
explanation. The Irishman is shrewd, and he will not toil in
the field, as the dumb beast does, without the prospect of
receiving at least some little portion of the harvest. He is the
hardest worker for a day's hire, that can be found, but it is
when the day's work brings a day's wages, even though they
be ever so small. But when, on the other hand, he sees that
all the profits of his toil go to another, and that other, perhaps, one that he hates, and has just reason for hating, then
he sits himself quietly down, and – looks around him!

J. VENEDEY, *Ireland and the Irish during the Repeal Year,* 1843

How Not To Be Poor

The struggle not just to survive, but if possible to escape from
misery, took various forms. Those best able to break their chains
were those who had a little surplus capital, or a little education, or
were less scrupulous than their fellow-countrymen.

Peasant Enterprise

25th April . . . In the evening I went with Patrick Shally . . . to see his holdings. We saw eight asses . . . I can recall when asses were so scarce that the horses would take fright whenever they saw one. A farmer called Mullaly, from near Callan, paid sixty pounds for a Spanish jack-ass two years ago, and gets a pound for every service . . .

HUMPHREY O'SULLIVAN, *Diary,* 1827
Trans. FRANK MURPHY

Mr Lanigan's School

Irish parents made great sacrifices so that their children could learn to read and write. Village or hedge schools like the one described here were a common feature of rural life in the 18th and early 19th centuries.

The school-house, at Glendalough, was situated near the romantic river which flows between the wild scenery of Drumgoff and the seven Churches. It was a low, stone building, indifferently thatched; the whole interior consisting of one oblong room, floored with clay, and lighted by two or three windows, the panes of which were patched with old copy-books, or altogether supplanted by school slates. The walls had once been plaistered and whitewashed, but now partook of that appearance of dilapidation which characterized the whole building . . . Along each wall were placed a row of large stones, the one intended to furnish seats for the boys, the other for the girls, the decorum of Mr Lanigan's establishment requiring that they should be kept apart. . . . The only chair in the whole establishment was that which was usually occupied by Mr Lanigan himself, and a table appeared to be a luxury of which they were either ignorant or wholly regardless . . .

The babble of a hundred voices, like the sound of a bee-hive, filled the house. Now and then, a school-boy, in frieze coat and corduroy trowsers, with an ink-bottle dangling at his breast, a copy-book, slate, Voster, and 'reading-book', under one arm, and a sod of turf under the other, dropped in, and took his place upon the next unoccupied stone. A great boy, with a huge slate in his arms, stood in the centre of the apartment, making a list of all those who were guilty of any indecorum in the absence of 'the Masther'. Near the door, was a blazing turf fire, which the sharp autumnal wind already rendered agreeable. In a corner behind the door lay a heap of fuel, formed by the contributions of all the schollars, each being obliged to bring one sod of turf every day, and having the privilege of sitting by the fire while his own sod was burning. Those who failed to pay their tribute of fuel sat cold and shivering the whole day long at the further end of the room, huddling together their bare and frost bitten toes, and casting a longing, envious eye toward the peristyle of well-marbled shins that surrounded the fire.

Full in the influence of a cherishing flame, was placed the hay-bottomed chair that supported the person of Mr. Henry Lanigan, when that great man presided in person in his rural seminary. On his right, lay a close bush of hazel, of astonishing size, the emblem of his authority and the instrument of castigation. Near this was a wooden 'sthroker', that is to say, a large rule of smooth and polished deal, used for 'sthroking' lines in copy-books, and also for 'sthroking' the palms of the refractory pupils. On the other side, lay a lofty heap of copy-books, which were left there by the boys and girls for the purpose of having their copies 'sot' by 'the Masther' . . .

It was the custom at Lanigan's academy, as it is at most Irish seminaries of a similar description, that no one should be permitted to leave the precincts of the school-room without taking with them a huge bone (the femur of a horse) which lay for that purpose in the centre of the floor, and which, on account of the privilege of furlough which it conferred, was designated by the name of The Pass.

GERALD GRIFFIN, *The Rivals*, 1830

The Smuggling Business

The safe and deep bays into which this coast [of Connemara] is cut, as well as the freedom from fear of customs officials, accounts for the presence of a number of people who are here for what is called quite openly the 'smuggling business', as if it were an ordinary trade. I have gone into different cabins and asked, straight away, for brandy or claret without finding any surprise to be expressed. One good woman, like many others, said to me, 'There is nothing at present in the house, but my husband is at sea, and if you come back in a month you can have all you want.'

DE LA TOCNAYE, *Promenade d'un Français dans l'Irlande,* 1797

Stealing

They steal every thing they can lay their hands on – and I should remark, that this is an account which has been very generally given me: all sorts of iron, hinges, chains, locks, keys, &c. – gates will be cut in pieces, and conveyed away in many places as fast as built; trees as big as a man's body, and that would require ten men to move, gone in a night. Lord Longford has had the new wheels of a car stolen as soon as made. Good stones out of a wall will be taken for fire-hearth, &c. though a breach is made to get at them. In short, every thing, and even such as are apparently of no use to them – nor is it easy to catch them, for they never carry their stolen goods home, but to some bog-hole. Turneps are stolen by car loads; and two acres of wheat pluckt off in a night. In short, their pilfering and stealing is a perfect nuisance! How far it is owing to the oppression of laws aimed solely at the religion of these people, how far to the conduct of the gentlemen and farmers, and how far to the mischievous disposition of the people themselves, it is impossible for a passing traveller to ascertain.

ARTHUR YOUNG, *A Tour in Ireland,* 1776–79

The Better Part of Valour

In a society where, to quote a famous judgement of the 18th century, 'the law does not suppose any such person to exist as an Irish Roman Catholic', the mass of the population had virtually no redress against injustice except isolated acts of revenge under cover of darkness. Economically powerless, deprived of legal rights, the Irish peasant had no choice but to show that he knew his place, at least in the daytime. The servility which he displayed before his masters, one of the skills necessary for his self-preservation, soon became second nature.

Oppression

The landlord of an Irish estate, inhabited by Roman Catholicks, is a sort of despot who yields obedience, in whatever concerns the poor, to no law but that of his will ... [He] can scarcely invent an order which a servant labourer, or cottar dares to refuse to execute. Nothing satisfies him but an unlimited submission. Disrespect or any thing tending towards sauciness he may punish with his cane or his horsewhip with the most perfect security; a poor man would have his bones broke if he offered to lift his hand in his own defence. Knocking down is spoken of in the country in a manner that makes an Englishman stare. Landlords of consequence have assured me that many of their cottars would think themselves honoured by having their wives and daughters sent for to the bed of their master; a mark of slavery that proves the oppression under which such people must live. Nay, I have heard anecdotes of the lives of people being made free with, without any apprehension of the justice of a jury. But let it not be imagined that this is common; formerly it happened every day, but law gains ground. It must strike the most careless traveller to see whole strings of cars whipt into a ditch by a gentleman's footman, to make way for his carriage; if they are over-turned or broken in pieces, no matter, it is taken in patience; were they to complain they would perhaps be horse-whipped.

ARTHUR YOUNG, *A Tour in Ireland*, 1776–79

Peelers

The Consequences of Revolt

Collectively as well as individually, the ruling class was swift to retaliate if the lower orders challenged its authority. In general it was able to keep the sullen peasantry in line through the courts, which it controlled; in an emergency, or to terrify the natives, landlords knew they could count on the local militia, whose members were not always noted for being squeamish. The following letter describes the summary justice awaiting those who challenged the established order, or seemed disloyal. It dates from the late 18th century when, inspired by the French Revolution, the Society of United Irishmen, which sought the setting up of an Irish republic, attracted many Irish peasants.

Moyvore, June 23rd, 1797.

Dear James,

To my great grief and sorrow I have to inform you of the untimely end of your two brothers, and alas! deprived [sic] me of a good husband. It is tedious to insert all the miseries the enemies to United Irishmen has brought on this neighbourhood, but particularly on the town of Moyvore, where there were forty houses and tenements burned, and levelled to the ground, on Monday night last, totally, by a boy of Patt. Ward's, who was taken for robbery, and to avoid being shot, turned informer, and brought in guilty and innocent. He first discovered where there was arms found, and when that was found true, they gave his speech credit afterwards. The same day, after shooting three men, the father and two sons, where they found the arms, they took poor Jack and Harry, together with one Mick Murray, and when they could not get any information from them, after getting the rites of the church, they were shot on Ballymore green. We waked them in the Chapel of Moyvore, when no man dare go near us – and applied to the Scullys, to shew us where we would bury them in Moranstown, and not one of them would come near us – nor could we get one to carry them, until Pat. Flanegan gave us a bed to carry them to Templeougra, where we buried them. Harry's little effects were saved, but on account of my going backward and forward to Ballymore, all my effects were consumed to ashes, as there was no one to carry them out. So, my dear friend, I have no shelter here, and I will impatiently wait your answer, or if you can afford me any relief, let me know it, as poor Jack relied on you to relieve his children – so no more at present from your poor disconsolate widow, who subscribes herself your loving sister-in-law.

MARY SMITH
Published in *The Press*, 9th January 1798

'Rebels destroying a house and furniture' during the uprising of 1798. Engravings like this one did much to create the image of 'Paddy' as a coarse, drunken half-wit.

A Letter from 'The Liberator'

In this letter written to his land-agent John Primrose during an outbreak of Asiatic cholera, Daniel O'Connell shows a fatherly concern for 'his' poor people of Derrynane, the O'Connell family seat.

London, 3rd March, 1834.

My dear John,

A far as as I am concerned, spare no expense that can possibly alleviate the sufferings of the people. You had better at once get Maurice O'Connor from Tralee, so as to have one medical man in Cahirciveen, and another to go to the country villages or single houses, wherever the disorder [cholera] appears. If it breaks out at all about Darrynane, Dr. O'Connor should go there at once to give the people every possible assistance. I will pay him readily 2 guineas a day while he is in the country. Do not delay, my dear John. Everybody should live as full as possible, eating meat twice a day. Get meat for the poor as much as possible. I wish my poor people about Darrynane should begin a meat diet before the disorder arrives among them. Two, three, four beeves I should think nothing of. Coarse blankets also may be very useful if got for them promptly. Could you not get coals from Dingle? If not, get them from Cork. In short, if I could contribute to save one life I would deem it a great blessing at the expense of a year's income. I spoke to Mr. Roche [a neighbouring land-agent]; he will write this day to Mr. Sullivan of Cove [the sub-agent] to give Father O'Connell £20 for that parish, particularly for Hartopp's tenants. But a physician is most wanting. Give me the fullest details; but above and before all other things, *be prodigal* of relief out of my means – beef, bread, mutton, medicines, physician, everything you can think of. Write off to Father O'Connell to take every previous precaution – a mass every possible day and getting the people to go to confession and communion, rosaries and other public prayers to avert the Divine Wrath.

Yours most affectionately,
Daniel O'Connell

Famine

The famine of 1845–51 is not the only one in Irish history; in the dreadful famine of 1740, for example, tens of thousands perished. But nothing in their long experience of hunger had prepared the Irish for what befell them when the potato crop failed several years in succession. One person in ten, or more than 800 000, died of hunger, or more commonly, of typhus, cholera, or another attendant disease. In the space of seven years (1845–51), more than a million and a half people emigrated. Thousands of bog Irish, many of them Irish-speaking, were to be found in the second half of the 19th century sweating in the textile mills of Northern England, or navvying in New South Wales, or serving in the Indian army, or building the railways of North America. It is perhaps the supreme irony of their nation's history that, through the diaspora which bled their own land white, these Irish played a vital part in building the British Empire, as much literally as figuratively, and in helping to make the language of their ancestral foe so widely spoken. No doubt, as they called to mind those who had not survived, they considered themselves lucky.

An Old Man Remembers

I remember one day, when I was about eight years old, standing near the rickyard. I saw a woman coming down the hill towards me. She was barefooted. She was walking at an even pace, but her breath was that of someone running. Her mouth was open so that I could see her teeth, and she was puffing. But the thing that struck me most of all was her legs: they were so swollen that each of them, from the knee down, was as big and as broad as a gallon container. This sight burned so deeply into my mind that I can still see it as clearly now as I did then, even though it was sixty-five years ago. This woman knew neither want nor distress till the blight came on the potatoes.

CANON PETER O'LEARY, *My Story*, 1915
Trans. FRANK MURPHY

A Visit to Skibbereen

On Christmas Eve, 1846, *The Times* of London published this letter, in which a Cork magistrate relates what he saw when visiting the village of Skibbereen, Co. Cork, nine days earlier. The letter is a copy of one which the magistrate, Nicholas Cummins, also sent to the Duke of Wellington.

My Lord Duke,

Without apology or preface, I presume so far to trespass on Your Grace as to state to you, and by the use of your illustrious name, to present to the British public the following statement of what I have myself seen within the last three days. Having for many years been intimately connected with the western portion of the County of Cork, and possessing some small property there, I thought it right personally to investigate the truth of several lamentable accounts which had reached me, of the appalling state of misery to which that part of the country was reduced. I accordingly went on the 15th instant to Skibbereen, and to give the instance of one townland which I visited, I shall state simply what I saw there . . . Being aware that I should have to witness scenes of frightful hunger, I provided myself with as much bread as five men could carry, and on reaching the spot I was surprised to find the wretched hamlet apparently deserted. I entered some of the hovels to ascertain the cause, and the scenes which presented themselves were such as no tongue or pen can convey the slightest idea of. In the first, six famished and ghastly skeletons, to all appearances dead, were huddled in a corner on some filthy straw, their sole covering what seemed a ragged horsecloth, their wretched legs hanging about, naked above the knees. I approached with horror, and found by a low moaning they were alive – they were in fever, four children, a woman and what had once been a man. It is impossible to go through the detail. Suffice it to say, that in a few minutes I was surrounded by at least 200 such phantoms, such frightful spectres as no words can describe, either from famine or from fever. Their demoniac yells are still ringing in my ears, and their horrible images are fixed upon my brain. My heart sickens at the recital, but I must go on.

In another case, decency would forbid what follows, but it must be told. My clothes were nearly torn off in my endeavour to escape from the throng of pestilence around, when my neckcloth was seized from behind by a grip which compelled me to turn, I found myself grasped by a woman with an infant just born in her arms and the remains of a filthy sack across her loins – the sole covering of herself and baby. The same morning the police opened a house on the adjoining lands, which was observed shut for many days, and two frozen corpses were found, lying upon the mud floor, half devoured by rats.

A mother, herself in a fever, was seen the same day to drag out the corpse of her child, a girl about twelve, perfectly naked, and leave it half covered with stones. In another house, within 500 yards of the cavalry station at Skibbereen, the dispensary doctor found seven wretches lying unable to move, under the same cloak. One had been dead many hours, but the others were unable to move either themselves or the corpse.

NICHOLAS CUMMINS, in a letter to *The Times*, published 24th December 1846

A New Song on the Rotten Potatoes

You landlords of Ireland I'd have you beware,
And of your poor tenants I wish you'd take care;
For want of potatoes in the present year
From the crutch to the cradle [they] are trembling with fear.

See how starvation meets us in the face,
But relief is expected from each foreign place.
Come, sell all your cattle and don't keep a tail
Before that you part with your corn or meal.

Through Ireland the potatoes do rot in the field,
If you were to see them it would make your heart bleed;
If they don't get relief, then the poor must prevail
And fight till they die for their corn and meal.

Then next try the landlords and see what they'll do,
For they know the potatoes are rotten all through;
Tell them for your rent that you'll give them good bail
Before that you'll part with your corn or meal.

*Iron pot for boiling potatoes and basket for straining
and serving them*

If then to your wishes they will not comply
Then tell them at once that you'd rather to die,
For your family is starving for want of the grain,
Then why should you part with your corn or meal?

There are some of those landlords playing their pranks
And sending the tenants to draw on their banks,
They'll have them like foxes all caught by the tail,
And then you must part with your corn & meal.

Let the Whigs and Repealers all join heart and hand,
And likewise the Tories to come on one plan,
To boldly come forward and never to fail,
And then we will have both our corn and meal.

Come cheer up good people, you need never fear,
For the rents they must fall upon this present year,
Sure they can't tyrannize or attempt to prevail
To make you to part with either corn or meal.

Do not be down-hearted, but cheer up once more,
The provision is coming from each foreign shore,
Good beer, flour and butter, rich sugar and tea,
From Russia and Prussia and Amerikay.

The potatoes have failed since the year forty-five;
The labour will flourish and trade will revive,
Public works and railroads will commence without fail,
And then we can purchase both corn and meal.

So now my good people, you need never fear,
Old Ireland will prosper on this present year,
But instead of potatoes believe what I say,
We'll have a cheap loaf with a good cup of tea.

                                        Broadsheet of 1847

DEATH

A funeral

Then, as now, the ultimate outcome of the struggle to survive was never in doubt. We know a good deal about the Irish approach to death in the 18th and early 19th centuries, as it was a common subject in the writing of the time. Were they a morbid lot, as has been suggested? Or were they simply less afraid to face reality than we are?

A Burial in Clonmel

It may be useful to recall that churchyards, like the churches themselves, were the property of the established church, which did not allow Catholic priests to conduct services there.

Whilst we were in the Church-Yard [at Clonmel, Co. Tipperary], a Child was attended to its Grave with the Irish Howl; it surpris'd Us to see It put in the ground and cover'd up, without any Burial-Service, the Company returning home; upon Enquiry, it was the Child of a Catholic, and the Protestant Service is never read over Them in this Kingdom.

JOHN LOVEDAY, *Diary of a Tour*, 1732

A Wake near Thomastown

In the afternoon, at Goulding (where the Weather detain'd Us), We heard a strange Yell; and looking out, there was a Coffin, a white Sheet spread over it, attended by a good number of people to a Malt-house, opposite to our Inn. About 7 o' th' Clock I went into the place, everything was preparing for the Solemnity; at one end of the Room was a Table spread with a white Cloth, on it Candles lighted – and Spriggs of Rosemary, some stuck in Candlesticks etc. with a Plate of Half-Pence: on one side stood a Stool, on which a Bowl of Tobacco and Pipes; on t'other side [of] the Table was the Coffin on the Ground, the Lid off, but the Body cover'd; round about, sat Men, Women etc. This they call a Wake, or Waking a Corpse; the poorer Catholics always do this – in their own Cabbins, if large enough; but This of the Deceas'd not being so commodious, They borrow'd my Landlady's empty Malt-house; They smoke and howl interchangeably all night, sitting by the Corps; in the morning I'm told their Priest comes, and performs some ceremonies, and then They carry the Dead to its Grave, the Priest attending to the Church-Yard Gate. Every one that comes to the Wake, except very poor, pays his Half-Penny; the expence of the Candles and Tobacco is defray'd with this. I paid my Penny, for intruding, and was offer'd a Pipe of Tobacco. One Woman softly groaned out – alone, alone, alone.

JOHN LOVEDAY, *Diary of a Tour*, 1732

Death by Murder

The Funeral of Denis Kelly

Well into the 19th century, the old clan loyalties of the Irish remained so strong that they sometimes led to brawls and even pitched battles between opposing factions (or clans). In his book on pre-Famine Ireland, S. J. Connolly tells how in 1821, for example, at considerable risk to his person, the curate of Mallow went into the midst of two enemy factions and 'had a conversation with one of the parties, the O'Mahonys . . . He reasoned with, and eventually succeeded in inducing them to return home, which they did in a body of about 500'.* The funeral here described is of a man killed in one of these faction-fights.

The coffin was brought out from the house and placed upon four chairs before the door, to be keened; and, in the meantime, the friends and well-wishers of the deceased were brought into the room to get each a glass of whiskey, as a token of respect. I observed also, that such as had not seen any of Kelly's relations until then, came up, and shaking hands with them, said, 'I'm sorry for your loss!' This expression of condolence was uniform and the usual reply was, 'Thank you, Mat, or Jim!' with a pluck of the skirt, accompanied by a significant nod, to follow. They then got a due share of whiskey; and it was curious, after they came out, their faces a little flushed, and their eyes watery with the strong, ardent spirits, to hear with what heartiness and alacrity they entered into Denis's praises.

When he had been keened in the street, there being no hearse, the coffin was placed upon two handspikes which were fixed across, but parallel to each other under it. These were borne by

* S. J. Connolly, *Priests and People in Pre-Famine Ireland 1780-1845,* Gill and MacMillan, Ireland, 1982, p. 231.

two men, one at the end of each, with the point of it crossing his body a little below his stomach; in other parts of Ireland, the coffin is borne upon a bier on the shoulders, but this is more convenient and less distressing.

When we got out upon the road, the funeral was of great extent – for Kelly had been highly respected. On arriving at the merin which bounded the land he had owned, the coffin was laid down, and a loud and wailing keene took place over it. It was again raised, and the funeral proceeded in a direction which I was surprised to see it take, and it was not until an acquaintance of my brother's had explained the matter that I understood the cause of it. In Ireland when a murder is perpetrated, it is sometimes usual, as the funeral proceeds to the grave-yard, to bring the corpse to the house of him who committed the crime, and lay it down at his door, while the relations of the deceased kneel down, and, with an appalling solemnity, utter the deepest imprecations, and invoke the justice of heaven on the head of the murderer. This, however, is generally omitted if the residence of the criminal be completely out of the line of the funeral, but if it be possible, by any circuit, to approach it, this dark ceremony is never omitted. In cases where the crime is doubtful, or unjustly imputed, those who are thus visited come out, and laying their right hand upon the coffin, protest their innocence of the blood of the deceased, calling God to witness the truth of their asseverations; but, in cases where the crime is clearly proved against the murderer, the door is either closed, the ceremony repelled by violence, or the house abandonned by the inmates until the funeral passes . . .

The funeral again proceeded, and I remarked that whenever a strange passenger happened to meet it, he always turned back, and accompanied it for a short distance, after which he resumed his journey, it being considered unlucky to omit this usage on meeting a funeral. Denis's residence was not more than two miles from the churchyard, which was situated in the town where he had received the fatal blow. As soon as we had got on about half

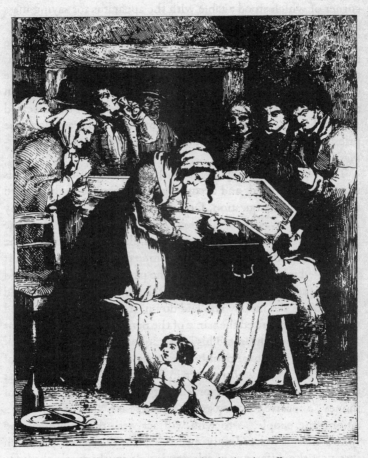

Mrs Kelly lamenting over her husband's coffin

of this way, the priest of the parish met us, and the funeral, after proceeding a few perches more, turned into a green field, in a corner of which stood a table with the apparatus for saying mass spread upon it.

The coffin was then laid down once more, immediately before this temporary altar; and the priest, after having robed himself, the wrong or sable side of the vestments out, as is usual in the case of death, began to celebrate mass for the dead, the congregation all kneeling. When this was finished, the friends of the deceased approached the altar, and after some private conversation, the priest turned round, and inquired aloud, 'Who will give *Offerings*?'

The people were acquainted with the manner in which this matter is conducted, and accordingly knew what to do. When the priest put the question, Denis's brother, who was a wealthy man, came forward, and laid down two guineas on the altar; the priest took this up, and putting it on a plate, set out among the multitude, accompanied by two or three of those who were best acquainted with the inhabitants of the parish. He thus continued putting the question, distinctly, after each man had paid; and according as the money was laid down, those who accompanied the priest pronounced the name of the person who gave it, so that all present might hear it. This is also done to enable the friends of the deceased to know not only those who show them this mark of respect, but those who neglect it, in order that they may treat them in the same manner on similar occasions. The amount of money so received is very great; for there is a kind of emulation among the people, as to who will act with most decency and spirit, that is exceedingly beneficial to the priest. In such instances the difference of religion is judiciously overlooked; for although the prayers of Protestants are declined on those occasions, yet it seems the same objection does not hold against their money, and accordingly they pay as well as the rest ...

When the offerings were all collected, the priest returned to the altar, repeated a few additional prayers in prime style – as rapid as lightning; and after hastily shaking the holy water on the crowd, the funeral moved on. It was now two o'clock, the day clear and frosty, and the sun unusually bright for the season. During mass, many were added to those who formed the funeral train at the outset; so that, when we got out upon the road, the procession appeared very large. After this, few or none joined it; for it is esteemed by no means 'dacent' to do so after mass, because, in that case, the matter is ascribed to an evasion of the offerings; but those whose delay has not really been occasioned by this motive, make it a point to pay them at the grave-yard, or after the interment, and sometimes even on the following day – so jealous are the peasantry of having any degrading suspicion attached to their generosity.

The order of the funeral now was as follows: – Foremost the women – next to them the corpse, surrounded by the relations – the eldest son, in deep affliction, 'led the coffin', as chief mourner, holding in his hand the corner of a sheet or piece of linen, fastened to the *mort-cloth*, called moor-cloth. After the coffin came those who were on foot, and in the rear were the equestrians. When we were a quarter of a mile from the church-yard, the funeral was met by a dozen of singing-boys, belonging to a chapel choir, which the priest, who was fond of music, had some time before formed. They fell in, two by two, immediately behind the corpse, and commenced singing the *Requiem*, or Latin hymn for the dead . . .

As we went up the street which had been the scene of the quarrel that proved so fatal to Kelly, the coffin was again laid down on the spot where he received his death-blow; and, as was usual, the wild and melancholy *keene* was raised . . .

At length, we entered the last receptacle of the dead. The coffin was now placed upon the shoulders of the son and brothers of the deceased, and borne round the churchyard; whilst the priest, with his stole upon him, preceded it, reading prayers for the eternal repose of the soul. Being then laid beside the grave, a 'De Profundis' was repeated by the priest and the mass-server; after which a portion of fresh clay, carried from the fields, was brought to his Reverence, who read a prayer over it, and consecrated it. This is a ceremony which is never omitted at the interment of a Roman Catholic. When it was over, the coffin was lowered into the grave, and the blessed clay shaken over it. The priest now took the shovel in his own hands, and threw in the three first shovelsful – one in the name of the Father, one in the name of the Son, and one in the name of the Holy Ghost. The sexton then took it, and in a short time Denis Kelly was fixed for ever in his narrow bed.

While these ceremonies were going forward, the churchyard presented a characteristic picture. Beside the usual groups who straggle through the place, to amuse themselves by reading the inscriptions on the tombs, you might see many individuals kneeling on particular graves, where some relation lay – for the benefit of whose soul they offered up their prayers with an attachment and devotion which one cannot but admire. Sometimes all the surviving members of the family would assemble, and repeat a Rosary for the same purpose. Again, you might see an unhappy woman beside a newly-made grave, giving way to lamentation and sorrow for the loss of a husband, or of some beloved child. Here, you might observe the 'last bed' ornamented with hoops, decked in white paper, emblematic of the virgin innocence of the individual who slept below; – there, a little board-cross informing you that 'this monument was erected by a disconsolate husband to the memory of his beloved wife' . . .

On the tombstones near Kelly's grave, men and women were seated, smoking tobacco to their very heart's content; for, with that profusion which characterises the Irish in everything, they had brought out large quantities of tobacco, whiskey, and bunches of pipes. On such occasions it is the custom, for those who attend the wake or the funeral to bring a full pipe home with them; and it is expected that, as often as it is used, they will remember to say, 'God be merciful to the soul of him that this pipe was over.'

WILLIAM CARLETON, *Traits and Stories of the Irish Peasantry*, 1830–33

Trial by Ordeal

It was . . . and is still the custom in most parts of Ireland, where any person is supposed to have 'come by his end' unfairly, that all the inhabitants of his parish, or district, particularly those who, from any previous circumstances, may be rendered at all liable to suspicion, shall meet together and undergo a kind of ordeal, by touching the corpse, each in his turn. Among a superstitious people, such a regulation as this, simple though it was, had been frequently successful in betraying the guilty conscience; and it was a current belief among the peasantry, that in many instances where the perpetrator of the horrid deed possessed strength of mind or callousness of heart sufficient to subdue all appearance of emotion in the moment of trial, some miraculous change in the corpse itself had been known to indicate the evil doer.

GERALD GRIFFIN, *Holland-tide,* 1827

Memorial cairns

Stones of Sorrow

A faint trail of Druidical superstition still lingers among the peasantry of Munster, where, if a murder has been committed in the
open air, it is considered indispensable in every Roman catholic
who passes by to throw a stone on the spot, which, from a strict
adhesion to this custom, presents a considerable pyramid of
stones. In the counties of Tipperary and Kerry, also, these stony
piles are to be found, which are beautifully and expressively
called clogh-breegh, or *stones of sorrow.*

JOHN CARR, *The Stranger in Ireland,* 1805

A Drowning in Dublin

A very disgusting circumstance occurred whilst I was in Dublin ... A
man was found drowned in the Liffey; he was taken up, and instead of
being taken to some bone-house to be owned, the body was exposed
in the street for two days, near the Queen's-bridge, upon straw, with a
plate of salt on his breast to excite the pity of passengers to place
money on it, for the purpose of appeasing the *manes* of the deceased
with a convivial funeral.

JOHN CARR, *The Stranger in Ireland,* 1805

Lord Clare's Funeral

John Fitzgibbon (1749–1802), Earl of Clare, was largely respon-
sible, as Lord Chancellor, for the passing of the Act of Union
which destroyed the last hope of an independant Ireland. This
earned him a lasting unpopularity; his nickname was 'Black
Jack'.

He died at his house in Ely-place, Dublin. An immense crowd
collected in the small street, in expectation of his funeral; and
the scene was a melancholy exhibition of some of those traits
which unfortunately mark the Irish as a peculiar people. In
every other nation, however uncivilized, there is a solemnity

attached to death which awes and, as it were, humanizes the heart, awakening a kindred feeling in all who contemplate the common lot of humanity. But with an excited Irish mob this impression is not made; death is no atonement for past offences, and the bitter feelings of prejudice and passion pursue the offender even in his grave. The mob assembled there was not the serious assemblage usual at a funeral. They were excited to yells and shrieks of the most appalling kind, curses loud and deep, and ribaldry the most revolting and disgusting. They followed the funeral procession to St. Peter's Church. It was hoped that the solemn sight of graves and coffins – the awful thought of death and judgement – would give some check to their passion. But no; they seemed to think the grave would only too soon shelter the body from them, and the earth would hide it before they had glutted their malice and revenge. They showered mud and dirt on the burial-place, and at last one ruffian hurled a dead cat on the coffin. Lord Clare was reputed to have used some expression to the effect that he would make the seditious as tame as domestic cats, and this ruffianly retort was received by the mob with shouts of applause.

JOHN EDWARD WALSH, *Ireland Sixty Years Ago*, 1847

The Death of Mary O'Sullivan

16th August At ten o'clock this morning my mother Mary Buckley O'Sullivan, wife of my father Donough O' Sullivan, passed away after making her last confession and being anointed, with the help of Almighty God. She was almost four score or eighty years of age. Her husband my father died in the year 1808, the year of the heavy snow. He is buried . . . a mile from Callan, although the family burial place is . . . near Killarney in County Kerry. But the trials of life, alas! separated us from our kinsfolk, thirty-six years ago . . .

17th August Fine autumn day. Wind from the north. While digging my mother's grave, I turned over in my mind many sad thoughts. There were the bones of my brother, who died thirty-one years ago, in the year 1796, mingled with the bones of my father, who died nineteen years ago, in the year 1808, and the bones of three of my children, the two Anastasias and little Humphrey, and who knows how long it will be before I am with them. My mother was buried at a quarter past six...

HUMPHREY O'SULLIVAN, *Diary,* 1827
Trans. FRANK MURPHY

Keens

Dr O'Brien, in his Irish dictionary (1768), describes the keen as 'a cry for the dead, according to certain loud and mournful notes, and verses, wherein the pedigree, land, property, generosity and good actions of the deceased person, and his ancestors, are diligently and harmoniously recounted, in order to excite pity and compassion in the hearers, and to make them sensible of their great loss in the death of the person whom they lament'.

Having a curiosity to hear the Keen more distinctly sung than over a corpse, when it is accompanied by a wild and inarticulate uproar as a chorus, I procured an elderly woman, who was renowned for her skill in keening, to recite for me some of these dirges. This woman, whose name was Harrington, led a wandering kind of life, travelling from cottage to cottage about the country, and though in fact subsisting on charity, found every where not merely a welcome, but had numerous invitations, on account of the vast store of Irish verses she had collected, and could repeat. Her memory was indeed extraordinary; and the clearness, quickness, and elegance with which she translated from the Irish into English, though unable to read or write, is almost incredible. Before she commenced repeating, she mumbled for a short time, probably the beginning of each stanza, to assure herself of the arrangement, with her eyes closed, rocking

Woman keening at a wake

her body backwards and forwards, as if keeping time to the measure of the verse. She then began in a kind of whining recitative, but as she proceeded and as the composition required it, her voice assumed a variety of deep and fine tones, and the energy with which many passages were delivered, proved her perfect comprehension and strong feeling of the subject, but her eyes always remained shut, perhaps to prevent interruption to her thoughts, or her attention being engaged by any surrounding object.

T. CROFTON CROKER, *Researches in the South of Ireland,* 1824

A Woman's Voice

With very rare exceptions, Irish writing in this period was domi-
nated by men. Keens however were sometimes composed by
women, as in these examples.

Oh John! Oh!

This is part of a keen on one John O'Brien, composed by his
sister.

> I will begin at the ground with thee.
> Thou hast two handsome legs,
> Two white thighs,
> A slender, chalk-like waist,
> Two broad shoulders,
> Pearly fine teeth,
> A cheek beauteously coloured,
> A fine gray eye –
> For which the women loved thee,
>   Oh John! Oh!

> Early 19th century
> Trans. JOHN O'DONOVAN

Lament for Art O'Leary

In 1773, a horse owned by one Captain Arthur O'Leary
aroused the envy of a Protestant landlord who, taking
advantage of the old penal law which forbade Catholics to
own a horse worth more than five pounds, tried to buy the
horse for this sum. O'Leary refused the offer, challenging the
landlord to a duel. He declined to fight the impetuous
officer, but later, apparently for self-protection, had
O'Leary shot down in an ambush. We would scarcely know
of this incident were it not that the Captain's wife, an aunt
of Daniel O'Connell, composed a keen in honour of her
dead husband, part of which is here translated.

I.

My love forever!
The day I first saw you
At the end of the market-house,
My eye observed you,
My heart approved you,
I fled from my father with you,
Far from my home with you.

II.

I never repented it:
You whitened a parlour for me,
Painted rooms for me,
Reddened ovens for me,
Baked fine bread for me,
Basted meat for me,
Slaughtered beasts for me;
I slept in ducks' feathers
Till midday milking-time
Or more if it pleased me.

III.

My friend forever!
My mind remembers
That fine spring day
How well your hat suited you,
Bright gold-banded,
Sword silver-hilted –
Right hand steady –
Threatening aspect –
Trembling terror
On treacherous enemy –
You poised for a canter
On your slender bay horse.
The Saxons bowed to you,

Down to the ground to you,
Not for love of you,
But for deadly fear of you,
Though you lost your life to them,
Oh my soul's darling.

IV.

Oh white-handed rider!
How fine your brooch was
Fastened in cambric,
And your hat with laces
When you crossed the sea to us,
They would clear the street for you,
And not for love of you
But for deadly hatred.

V.

My friend you were forever!
When they will come home to me,
Gentle little Conor
And Farr O'Leary, the baby,
They will question me so quickly,
Where did I leave their father.
I'll answer in my anguish
That I left him in Killnamartyr.
They will call out to their father:
And he won't be there to answer.

VI.

My friend and my love!
Of the blood of Lord Antrim,
And of Barry of Allchoill,
How well your sword suited you,

Hat gold-banded,
Boots of fine leather,
Coat of broadcloth,
Spun overseas for you.

VII.

My friend you were forever!
I knew nothing of your murder
Till your horse came to the stable
With the reins behind her trailing,
And your heart's blood on her shoulders
Staining the tooled saddle
Where you used to sit and stand.
My first leap reached the threshold,
My second reached the gateway,
My third leap reached the saddle.

VIII.

I struck my hands together
And I made the bay horse gallop
As fast as I was able,
Till I found you dead before me
Beside a little furze-bush.
Without Pope or bishop,
Without priest or cleric
To read the death-psalms for you,
But a spent old woman only
Who spread her cloak to shroud you –
Your heart's blood was still flowing;
I did not stay to wipe it
But filled my hands and drank it.

EIBHLIN DUBH O'CONNELL,1773
Trans. EILIS DILLON

Two lamentations

Wake Games

On the eve of burial, friends and relatives of the dead would gather at the house where the corpse lay, both to lament and to celebrate. The wake, as it was known, was an important social event which lasted all night, and included various customs and practices of obscure origin.

Short Castle

Amongst the games played at wakes, are two which I have never observed out of Ireland, and from their being so universal with the peasantry, they are probably of considerable antiquity. One of these is called 'the walls of Troy', and the other 'short castle'. Of the former, although I took some pains to acquire it, I now find myself

unable to give a satisfactory description; the latter is played on
lines (usually marked with chalk) in this form. Each player is

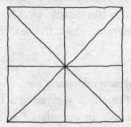

provided with three counters (small black and white pebbles, or
shells) which are singly deposited on the board in turn: the game is
won by getting these three counters in a straight line. The centre
point is considered the most advantageous, and is always taken by
the first player; when all the counters are deposited, moves are
made from one point to the next, should it be unoccupied, and so
on, unless a careless move on either side decides the game, by
allowing the adversary to form his three counters in a row.

T. CROFTON CROKER, *Researches in the South of Ireland*, 1824

A wake

The Frannsa

The drunkenness and licence which often marked these occasions were frowned on by the clergy, who had limited success in attempting to have them stopped. This text refers to the first part of the 19th century.

During [the Frannsa], several young men and women were married by a mock priest (usually a weaver or a tailor, called Roberd Sagart), who was generally in attendance at all the wakes in his parish, and who was the life and soul of the whole farce. He was usually dressed in robes made of straw; his stole was a huge sugaun made of oaten straw, and his vestments were made of the same material. He usually carried a huge Paidrin, or beads, made of potatoes of different sizes, on a string, surmounted by a huge frog for a cross. He commenced the profane ceremony by blessing himself with his left hand, and then repeated in Latin, 'Ego jungo vos in matrimonium,' etc. After each couple was married, he put them to bed in a corner of the room, sprinkling them with water, and pronouncing a mock blessing upon them in Latin and Irish – 'Crescite et multiplicamini,' and adding, 'Now that ye are joined in the holy bonds of matrimony, may the full blessing of the beggars descend upon you; may ye have plenty of ragged children,' etc. But this blessing was varied according to the genius and humour of the pseudo-priest, who sometimes gave the married couple plain advice about their future conduct as man and wife, and which was generally of so ludicrous a character as to create much laughter.

JOHN O'DONOVAN in *Transactions of the Kilkenny Archaeological Society*, 1858–59

Aghadoe Church

[We visited] Aghadoe Church (Co. Kerry) on the hillside, with such a populous cemetery; skulls and bones lying about, and sheep feeding among the tombs; yet it is a cheerful burying place, if one can imagine this seeming contradiction . . . In the interior of the old church, I saw a coffin; the lid was off, and within lay a form wrapped in now discoloured grave-clothes; about lay piled, broken coffins and bones, and one must shudder at such ghastly tokens of our mortality, and a stranger to the Irish character feel that in these exhibitions there must be a sort of disrespect to the dead. This is not the case. No nation respects their dead more – witness their wakes and funerals; and no nation loves more devotedly the grave, however humble, of their parents; and no nation believes more firmly in the promise of the resurrection! I asked a countryman as to why these bones and coffins were let lie about in that neglected manner, and he told me that every family had its little grave, and that when that was too full of coffins, the oldest coffin was taken up, to give place to the new. 'And sure,' he added, 'all the church-yard is holy ground, praise be to God!'

CATHERINE M. O'CONNELL, *Excursions in Ireland*, 1844

Joyce's Repentance

A reflection on death, this poem known simply as Peter Joyce's Repentance seems to come from Co. Mayo.

Deeply I sigh, and well I may,
  And dark is the day for one like me,
  For no-one knows, nor yet know I,
  Or whence, or why, or who I be.

I am a sinful man of men,
  Sin's iron pen my feet have trod;
  No single inch of me is whole,
  So long my soul hath fought with God.

The son of Grace, our priest and leech,
  (Alas for each who finds not Him!)

Now who shall wash my crimson stain,
Or lull the pain in every limb!

For sick and sore in branch and root,
My foot a direful course did trace,
Since first my heart, observed of none,
Began to shun the ways of grace.

Just when I think my soul to win,
I sin some sin, or lie some lie,
As ducks will leave the clearest springs
To daub their wings in pools half dry.

The fight with Death is hard and long:
(Though Death is strong his pace is slow);
Like helpless ships we turn and toss
And drift across the waves of woe.

Upon this hinge hangs all my dole,
My pain of soul, my bitter smart,
That I have warred with Him who brought
Me out of nought – rebellious heart!

Condemned was Adam, branch and root,
Who plucked the fruit that wrought the fall;
But I thrice five commandments break,
Nor take my sin to heart at all.

Once was I good, I once was pure,
Whilst yet the lure of sin lay hid;
But as I, ripening, slowly grew,
I lusted too for things forbid.

Gluttony, sloth, distemper, greed,
Led me with speed the deathly way;
Envy and anger, lust and strife,
Made of my life their hideous prey.

O man, my warning take to thee,
  That health shall flee, that youth shall part;
  That as I am, thou yet shall be,
  But ne'er again as now thou art.

I too was strong, I lived in peace
  Until my lease of life went by;
  A faggot now of wearied bones,
  Upon the stones of death I lie.

There came to meet me on my way,
  And not today, nor yesterday,
  A change of form, of voice, of face,
  And life's dear grace has passed away.

The prize of love from God I got,
  I thanked Him not, – now none is left;
  And flown are hearing, memory, sight,
  The foot so light, the hand so deft.

But in their hand have made a breach,
  Each after each, a loathly band,
  Deafness and lameness, causeless dread,
  Languor of head and palsied hand.

The sight has flown the feeble eyes,
  Their quickness flies the fingers deft;
  And all the weary body groans,
  And in the bones no sap is left.

Gaunt are the hollow cheeks and bare,
  And fallen the hair, a rueful sight;
  What once was bright is dark in me,
  And ne'er shall be again made bright.

Now says my wife, my children say,
  'Old man away! we heed not thee;

Deaf thou art, would that thou wert dumb,
May death now come and set thee free.'

My friends they think, nor lose one sigh,
  (And even I myself must say),
    That were my soul but sure of grace,
    The body's place were in the clay.

I pray O Lord, Thy will be mine,
  Since for my crime how shall I pay?
    The flesh afflict with ache and dole,
    But spare the soul, I meekly pray.

Aloud, aloud I call on Thee,
  Though bold I be on Thee to call,
    For in those years Thou gavest me,
    I wrought for Thee, ah! not at all.

A woe of woes is mine this day,
  For through my hay the wet winds blow,
    The swathes ungathered and undone, –
    And now the sun is sinking low.

O King of Heaven, my pride forgive,
  And let me live, till this old heart
    By perfect penitence be wrung,
    And stung by conscience wholesome smart.

Hearken my prayer, incline Thine ear,
  Now let the tear of grace flow free;
    The sinner finds (his brief hour run),
    Pity from none, but only Thee.

Thine is my life and Thine my death,
  God of all breath, my pride is o'er!
    One glance from Thee were all my wealth,
    My hope, my health, for evermore!

O Thou who makest dead to live,
  Who didst forgive the Thief his scorn,
  Hear now, as then, a sinner's sigh,
  The bitter cry of me forlorn.

O pierced in foot and hand and side,
  O crucified for hearts that burn,
  I turn to Thee, O turn to me,
  I ne'er again from Thee shall turn.

O King of Kings, O King of Worlds,
  O King who was, and is to be,
  Forgive O King, our world, and spare;
  Receive our prayer, and comfort me.

First half of 18th century (?)
Trans. DOUGLAS HYDE

Round tower of Kilree (Co. Kilkenny)

LOVE, MARRIAGE AND CHILDREN

A wedding feast

Such data as can be found indicates that throughout this period the population rose steadily, from something like a million in Cromwell's time to more than eight million just before the Famine. But if none would deny that the Irish were prolific, not everyone would describe them as an erotic people. In looking carefully, however, perhaps we can begin to see why thay have been called the Latins of the British Isles.

Temptation

As well as teaching in his school in Callan, Co. Kilkenny, Humphrey O'Sullivan also managed a draper's shop which seems to have belonged to his wife. He wrote this entry in this diary in 1827, when he was forty-seven years old.

18th April At midday, I went with merry sweet-voiced Margaret Barry [the daughter of a local widow] and another person to Desart Court following the same roads as Easter Sunday. We went through woods of dark, evergreen pines, along pretty lanes, now crooked and now straight, hidden from the sun, listening to the trilling of the larks on either side, the blackbird callling to his mate, the warble of the thrush, and other song-birds, as sweet-voiced as gentle Margaret Barry. We lost our way in a dark and secluded little glen, not knowing which way to go. Finally, making our way through mossy hollows and bramble thickets, sloping groves of ash and evergreen pines, we came to Cluain Lachan, with its ponds and pools, its streams, its murmuring waterfall. Here we found white ducks and speckled drakes, and blackbirds singing loudly on top of the white-thorn bushes.

'I'm tired,' said gentle sweet-voiced Margaret.

'So am I,' I said.

'Let's sit down on the moss.'

'Yes, let's.'

With the murmuring of the waterfall, Margaret fell asleep. Let the wind waft softly through the trees around the pond! Let there be perfect peace and calm! The wind blew softly through the hair of the sleeping wanderer, baring her neck as white as a swan. Her lips were as red as rowan-berries, as sweet as honey, her white bosom like two snowy hillocks, rising and falling like the waves of the Blackwater; her slender waist, her round little rump, her dainty legs hidden by the satin dress which came down to her firm feet.

Two snipe flew up from the pool into the air like arrows from a bow. The beautiful girl woke with a start.

'This pool has no equal in all Ireland!' I said. 'None whatsoever! The sun's beginning to set. Let's go home!'

We went home tired out, her arm in mine, her head on my shoulder, her eyes downcast. I cannot recall a more beautiful day.

HUMPHREY O'SULLIVAN, *Diary*, 1827
Trans. FRANK MURPHY

Peasant girls

Love Songs of Connaught

Passed from one generation to another, usually by word of mouth, these popular love songs are part of a collection which Douglas Hyde wrote down and translated into English at the end of the 19th century. Some were composed by women, a fact worth noting, as women's voices are almost never heard in Irish literature of this period.

I Shall Not Die for Thee

For thee I shall not die,
  Woman high of fame and name;
Foolish men thou mayest slay
  I and they are not the same.

Why should I expire
  For the fire of any eye,
Slender waist or swan-like limb.
  Is't for them that I should die?

Young men passing the time of day in Cork

The round breasts, the fresh skin,
  Cheeks crimson, hair so long and rich;
Indeed, indeed, I shall not die,
  Please God, not I, for any such.

The golden hair, the forehead thin,
  The chaste mien, the gracious ease,
The rounded heel, the languid tone,
  Fools alone find death from these.

Thy sharp wit, thy perfect calm,
  Thy thin palm like foam of sea;
Thy white neck, thy blue eye,
  I shall not die for thee.

Woman, graceful as the swan,
  A wise man did nurture me,
Little palm, white neck, bright eye,
  I shall not die for ye.

Traditional
Trans. DOUGLAS HYDE

The Brow of the Red Mountain

I am sitting up
  Since the moon rose last night,
And putting down a fire,
  And ever kindling it diligently;
The people of the house
  Are lying down, and I by myself.
The cocks are crowing,
  And the land is asleep but me.

O may I never leave the world
  Till I loose from me the ill-luck,
Till I have cows and sheep
  And my one desire of a boy.
I would not think the night long
  Lying by his smooth white breast,
And sure I would allow the race of Eve
  After that to say their choice thing of me.

Love covers up hate
  In every place in which there is beauty in a
woman;
On a high narrow bed
  For three long months I have lain,
Remembering my love
  That I left on the Brow of the Red Mountain,
Weeping my fill,
  My countenance wet with tears.
The 'black ale' [bitterness] I make,
  I cannot drink any of it;
And badly though I need it,
  I cannot get my sleep;
The curse of the Son of God upon the one
  Who took from me my love

And left me by myself,
  Each single long night in misery.

And oh, young boy,
  I'll not be mocked by you,
You have nothing to say,
  Except only that I am without a fortune.
You are not my love,
  And my destruction if I am sorry for it;
And if I am without a dowry of cattle,
  I am content to lie alone.

Traditional
Trans. DOUGLAS HYDE (adapted)

Irish Chastity

There are no more innocent girls in the world than the Irish girls
... One has but to walk through an English and Irish town, and
see how much superior is the morality of the latter. That great
terror-striker, the Confessional, is before the Irish girl, and
sooner or later her sins must be told there.

WILLIAM MAKEPEACE THACKERAY, *The Irish Sketch Book*, 1843

The Old Man's Tale

In the latter part of the 18th century, Brian Merriman, a Clareman,
wrote *The Midnight Court*, the last major work to be written in Irish
before the Famine. In this lengthy satire of about 1000 lines, he
ridiculed the hypocrisy of his day, especially that surrounding
relations between the sexes. Perhaps, as this extract suggests,
not all Irish girls were as chaste as Thackeray claimed.

The things I'm told, I could raise your hair
By recounting the times she's been stretched out bare,
On the flat of her back upon the ground
And the customers rushing from miles around.

From youth to grandad, all can speak
Of her adaptable technique –
In Ibrickane with big and small,
In Tirmaclane with one and all,
In Kilbrickane with thick and thin,
In Clare, in Ennis and in Quin,
In Cratlee and Tradree where they're tough
She never seemed to have enough!
But I'd still have allowed her a second chance
And blamed it on youthful extravagance
Were it not that I saw with my own two eyes
On the roadway – naked to the skies –
Herself and a lout from the Durrus bogs
Going hammer and tong like a couple of dogs.

BRIAN MERRIMAN (1749-1805), *The Midnight Court*
Trans. DAVID MARCUS

Brian Merriman (1749–1805)

Two Weddings

Throughout much of this period, Catholic weddings, as well as baptisms, were customarily performed in private houses.

Late 17th Century

Mrs. Browne being invited she carried us with her to the house where the kindred of the young folks were all met together, and the priest of the parish, without whom nothing could be done on this occasion. The bride was clad in a red frieze petticoat and waist coat with green tape about the skirts; on her head she wore a white hood of linen, for they do not wear the kercher until they are married, and she sat in a dark corner of the room with two or three other young women about her. The bridegroom was a strapping young fellow with a grey frieze suit on; he had brogues on his feet, and [li]ned leather gloves, and a long neck cloth about his neck, as long as any of our steenkirks, and a blue ribbon in his hat. The priest began the ceremony by asking the man, Will you take Nora here present for your lawful wife according to the rites of holy mother church? . . .

Then the bridegroom laid some small pieces of silver for the Arrha, with the ring (which was made of a small twig of an osier handsomely plaited) on the book. Then the priest blessed the ring with two crosses and a short prayer, after which he sprinkled holy water upon it in form of a cross. Then he delivers it to the man, who holding the woman's right hand in his left says, With this ring I thee wed etc., as we do; then he puts it on the tip of the woman's thumb saying In the name of the father, then on the fore-finger and says Of the son, then on the middle finger saying And of the Holy Ghost, and lastly on the ring finger where he leaves it saying Amen; and after a few other prayers the business is done. The ring was taken off by one of the young women who I suppose was a sort of bridesmaid, and tied on one of the strings of the bride's purse which hung at her girdle, and it is either worn there or in the bridegroom's hatband until it is either broken or lost. Then liquor went about to all the guests wishing *health, wealth and prosperity* to the young couple. At supper the bride sat at the upper end of the table, and Father James the priest at the right hand. He was a jolly fellow that loved to be much made of, and pretended to be a great traveller ...

After supper Father James desired to do his last office, which was to bless the genial bed, and accordingly everything being ready, he was carried into a room which was divided by a wattled partition plastered with clay from the room we were in. It had a wattled door which was not impervious to Argus eyes, and made rather to keep out the swine or the calves than for either privacy or warmth.

He began saying, Our help is in thee, O Lord, who made heaven and earth. The Lord be with you. To which he was answered, And with your spirit. Then he prayed thus, Bless O Lord this bed, that all lying in it may rest in thy peace, and preserve and grow old in observance of thy will, and multiply in length of days, and at last arrive at the Kingdom of Heaven, Amen.

Then he besprinkled it and all the room with holy water which he had brought with him for the nonce; and so his part of the show ended, and exit priest ...

I forgot to tell you that after the matrimonial ceremony was over we had a bag piper and a blind harper that dinned us with their music, to which there was perpetual dancing; only whilst we were at supper and blessing the bed.

JOHN DUNTON, *Teague Land, or a Merry Ramble to the Wild Irish,* 1698

Early 19th Century

We ... proceeded to the room where the company were assembled. The floor was earthern, but clean. A table was decently laid out for dinner. I was introduced to the bride. She was a modest-looking girl about seventeen. She was dressed in a white calico gown and ribands, and had a fan in her hand. The Priest now began the ceremony. The evening was close and the

A Kerry husband bringing home his bride

room crowded. He soon got into a violent heat, and to cool himself, took his wig off several times, wiped his head, and replaced it [*sic*] But whatever there might be uncouth in his manner, there was nothing ludicrous, either in that of the bride or her parents . . .

After the ceremony was over, the whiskey went around, and we then sat down to dinner. It was a very abundant one, not ill-dressed, – nor, considering the condition of the people, ill-served. The priest was grand carver, grand talker too, and grand laugher . . .

The moment dinner was over, the table was removed, and the company began dancing. The dances were reels of three and of four – when one person got tired, another instantly started up in his or her place, and the best dancer was he or she who held out the longest. A singular kind of *pas seul* was performed by a *crack* dancer. A door was taken off the hinges, and laid on the floor, on which he danced in his stocking-soles. He displayed considerable activity, but there was an almost total lack of grace. His principal movement consisted in rapidly and alternately raising his feet as

high as his waistcoat, and when he succeeded in getting his toes a
little way into the pocket, there was a universal burst of
applause.

J. GAMBLE, *A View of Society and Manners in the North of Ireland*, 1812

An Unforgettable Wedding Night

In this extract from his renowned satire, Merriman describes the
anguish of a young bride on the night of her wedding to an
elderly man.

A starved old gelding, blind and lamed
And a twenty-year-old with her parts untamed.
It wasn't her fault if things went wrong.
She closed her eyes and held her tongue;
She was no ignorant girl from school
To whine for her mother and play the fool
But a competent bedmate smooth and warm
Who cushioned him like a sheaf of corn.
Line by line she bade him linger
With gummy lips and groping finger,
Gripping his thighs in a wild embrace
Rubbing her brush from knee to waist
Stripping him bare to the cold night air,
Everything done with love and care.
But she'd nothing to show for all her labour;
There wasn't a jump in the old deceiver,
And all I could say would give no notion
Of that poor distracted girl's emotion,
Her knees cocked up and the bedposts shaking,
Chattering teeth and sinews aching,
While she sobbed and tossed through a joyless night
And gave it up with the morning light.

BRIAN MERRIMAN (1749-1805), *The Midnight Court*
Trans. FRANK O'CONNOR

Have You Been at Carrick?

In the mid-19th century, as they sailed to the United States or Australia, Irish-speaking peasants no doubt sang or hummed snatches from the songs of the day, many of which reflected the romantic fashion of the period. Florid and even tedious as it may seem to us, the style of this song is typical of much Irish verse of the 18th and early 19th centuries.

I.

Have you been at Carrick, and saw you my true-love there?
And saw you her features, all beautiful, bright, and fair?
Saw you the most fragrant, flowering, sweet apple-tree? –
O! saw you my lov'd one, and pines she in grief like me?

II.

I have been at Carrick, and saw thy own true-love there;
And saw, too, her features, all beautiful, bright, and fair;
And saw the most fragrant, flowering, sweet apple-tree –
I saw thy lov'd one – she pines not in grief, like thee!

III.

Five guineas would price every tress of her golden hair –
Then think what a treasure her pillow at night to share,
These tresses thick-clustering and curling around her brow –
O, Ringlet of Fairness! I'll drink to thy beauty now!

IV.

When seeking to slumber, my bosom is rent with sighs –
I toss on my pillow till morning's blest beams arise;
No aid, bright Beloved! can reach me save God above,
For a blood-lake is form'd of the light of my eyes with love!

V.

Until yellow Autumn shall usher the Paschal day,
And Patrick's gay festival come in its train alway –

Until through my coffin the blossoming boughs shall grow,
My love on another I'll never in life bestow!

VI.

Lo! yonder the maiden illustrious, queen-like, high,
With long-flowing tresses adown to her sandal-tie –
Swan, fair as the lily, descended of high degree,
A myriad of welcomes, dear maid of my heart, to thee!

Trans. EDWARD WALSH

The Married State

The grim realism of the Irish peasantry is perhaps best seen in their traditional tales. Here, with shrewd terseness, the married state is often shown as one of constant warfare between man and wife.

The Woman and the Two Geese

There was a couple long ago who had an invitation to a wedding. They went, and on their way they came upon a large puddle of water on the road. A goose was swimming on the puddle, and the woman said to her husband that there were two geese there.

'Ah, close your mouth, foolish woman,' said the man to her, 'Don't you see that that's the reflection underneath and the goose swimming above?'

The woman insisted that there were two geese there, and he said that there was only one goose.

'There are two geese,' she said to him again.

'I can see that it's no good arguing with you,' said the man to her.

So on they went to the wedding and were made welcome there, but whenever the man spoke to his wife, she said that there were two geese, and he replied that there was only one. She said there were two. So the man was embarrassed, probably, and he told her to come home with him, and they walked home together, and she lay down to rest on reaching home, and he told her after a while to get up and look after the children. She said to him that there were two geese, and he said that there was only one. She said there were two. Finally she lay on her death-bed, and the neighbours gathered and he told her father and mother and all her people, and every one of them came to weep over her, and when they had all done weeping, 'Go home now,' he said to them, 'and weep for the mother of my children.'

He wept and whispered to her. 'Ah, get up, Mary,' he said to her, 'and tell me you're just lying down or weak, and take care of the children.'

'There were two geese there.' said Mary.

'There was only one,' said he.

'There were two,' Mary said to him.

So they were going to put her into the coffin, and he told them to wait a little, while he wept over her before she was put into the coffin. He stood near her and wept over her, and as he wept, he told her to get up now, for they were ready to put her into the coffin and carry her off to the churchyard.

She said to him that there were two geese, and he said that there was only one.

'There were two geese there,' she said.

So they carried her off to the churchyard and buried her, and the husband went home alone. The next day he came back to the churchyard and opened the grave and took the lid off the coffin.

'Are you alive, Mary?' he asked.

Mary said to him, 'There were two geese there.'

'I give in, it's no good arguing with you,' he said. 'Get up for God's sake, and come home.'

She went home, and he never said another word about the geese from that day on.

That is my story, and if there is a lie in it, let it be.*

Traditional tale
Trans. FRANK MURPHY

---

* This formula is often found at the end of folktales.

John the Miser

John's desire was to be richer than any of his neighbours. His father and mother had left him a great fortune – gold and silver, cattle, sheep and horses. He refused to marry any of the local girls, unless he could find a wife who ate nothing, and he withered with age and with depriving himself of proper food and clothing.

There was a sporting, respectable girl who knew how to say and do the right thing to make people happy, but she had not even a penny for her dowry. She said to John, 'I would suit you well, for I have never eaten a thing all my life, and I will not eat as long as I live. What wealth we will have if we marry and save together.'

John agreed and said, 'Clare, be ready tomorrow and we'll go to the priest's house, and the match will be made.'

Clare was ready. John arrived with the best man. Clare and John were married that very day.

When they came home, John said to Clare, 'You should eat something tonight, Clare.'

'But I've already told you,' said Clare, 'that I've never eaten a thing all my life, and never will.'

Ah! John was overjoyed. For the next few months Clare ate all she wanted without John knowing, and she said to him, 'You should learn how not to eat, and see how much richer we'll be.'

'But how?' asked John. 'How can I learn?'

'Take your pick-axe in the morning,' replied Clare. 'Keep your head bent over your work as you dig up the road outside. If you think of eating before evening, try to think of something else, and get rid of the idea.'

John did as she had said. He came home in the evening and said, 'Clare, I'm weak.'

'Go to bed quickly,' said Clare, 'and think of the progress you've made.'

John went to sleep, and in the morning was even weaker.

'Stay in bed today,' said Clare. He stayed, and on the third day John was close to death. Clare sent for the priest to come and administer Extreme Unction.

She took a big turkey that was in the house, killed it, and put it in the pot to cook. When it was cooked, she began to eat it while John lay dying on the bed in front of her.

'Will you eat that?' John asked her.

'I will eat it,' she answered, 'every single bit.'

'Oh!' said John mimicking her, broken-hearted, 'every single bit! every single bit! every single bit!' When the priest came, he asked, 'What's the matter, my good sir?'

John replied, 'Every single bit! Every single bit!'

'What's this he's saying?' the priest asked Clare.

She answered, 'He was afraid that he would die before you came, and he told me to tell you, "Every single bit that I own, I leave to you".'

'And I won't interfere with that,' said the priest.

John did not recover, but worsened and died before the priest left the house. Clare is wealthy now that the miser is dead.

Traditional tale
Trans. FRANK MURPHY

Scutching flax

Children

Ode on the Birth of a Son

Though not of great merit, this little ode gives some idea of the
occasional verse which Irish poets 'churned out' to mark births,
marriages and deaths in important families. The translator, Brian
O'Looney, was one of the last Irish scribes.

John Hore Sang
On the Birth of Charles MacDonnell of
Kilkee in 1736

A branch of the glorious tree
  Is this visitor in Kilbrickan,
Whom the Son of God hath sent in our way
  With power from the king of grace.
Blessed is that young lady
  In whose womb the babe was formed,
The blooming branch of Fódla,
  Drinking the streams from the breasts of Tail.

By the free clans of nobles, in chorus while drinking
  One thousand and one huzzas have been raised,
Into the vaults of heaven, greeting Charles,
  My lion's worthy son,
They've punch and wine draining there,
  And also plenteous beer,
And the blood-red bonfires blazing,
  Most sportingly before us.

Fix him in a golden cradle,
  Give him a kiss and flow to him the breast milk,
Sit and sing for him a lullaby,
  Melodious and tastefully sweet.
Ne'er let him get a crying fit,

Or a tear down from his eye;
He's kin to Brian Boru,
   Who made Fódla obey his laws.

He's kin to Brian, son of Bruadar,
   Who was of the old nobility;
He's kin to Thomond's Earl,
   At this time called Inchiquin;
Kin to the sportive troop,
   And to the lordly chief of Dough;
And he in chieftainship excelled
   All ye who went from us into the armies of
[King] Louis.

JOHN HORE, 1736
Trans. BRIAN O'LOONEY

Children at a mill-grate

Children, Children Everywhere

After a couple of months in the country, the stranger's eye grows
somewhat accustomed to the rags: they do not frighten him as at
first; the people who wear them look for the most part healthy
enough: especially the small children – those who can scarcely
totter, and are sitting shading their eyes at the door, and leaving
the unfinished dirt-pie to shout as the coach passes by – are as
healthy a looking race as one will ever see. Nor can any one pass
through the land without being touched by the extreme love of
children among the people: they swarm everywhere, and the
whole country rings with cries of affection towards the children,
with the songs of young ragged nurses dandling babies on their
knees, and warnings of mothers to Patsey to come out of the mud,
or Norey to get off the pig's back.

WILLIAM MAKEPEACE THACKERAY, *The Irish Sketch Book*, 1843

Politeness

The manner which [*sic*] the children of the peasantry answer any
question is quite pleasant. They never say 'yes' or 'no', but 'I have
not, ma'am', 'I will, ma'am', 'I do, ma'am', 'I do not, ma'am', etc.

A. NICHOLSON, *The Bible in Ireland*, 1844–45

Sauciness

Many strangers have complained of the annoyance of [children]
following them, but we found more of the ludicrous than the
disagreeable in our 'tail'. Our attempts to dissuade them from
accompanying the party were quite unavailing, and . . . M- tried
his powers of eloquence in a rather lengthened oration, proving
the mischief of idleness, the comfort of employment. A smart
black-eyed nymph, evidently *l'enfant gâtée* of the troop, saucily
replied, 'Sure, your honour, we work all the winter and the
spring, and, like the quality, we take our divarshion in the fine
weather'.

CATHERINE O'CONNELL *Excursions in Ireland*, 1844

Mother and child

Mother and Son

It is impossible to overrate, in describing, the devoted attachment of Irish mothers to their children – to their sons especially; they sometimes speak harshly and snappishly to their daughters, but their boys are petted and spoiled as much as boys can well be: this is the case throughout the country. No matter what privations the poor mother endures, she shields her child without considering herself. Is her pillow of twisted straw? she cherishes him in her bosom. Is the wind high, and does the hail fall? she kneels down like the camel in the desert, and the children who have been trotting by her hand or gallopping before her, climb on her back, and cling there, sheltered from the storm by their mother's cloak, who breasts the tempest with her burden. Is the food scant?

with a sad yet patient countenance she divides the potatoes, reserving to herself the scraps and skins which an English dog would refuse. The consequence is, that whatever it may be towards the father, the love of the boy is with the mother. And this is apparent in all things: when she grows old, the mother of the husband rules, not only him, but his house and his wife; and young girls have always a great dread of 'the mother-in-law over them'; but in their turn they rule, and with the same power and the same results. As to the daughters, you frequently hear the observation, 'Augh, sure she has got a husband, and she must put up with his quareness, as we had to do with the man that owned us: glory be to God! but they are all mighty quare for men every one of them – mighty quare intirely!' But for the son: 'Oh then, sure my boy – and a fine boy he was – might have done far better than taking up with her; not that there's anything against her, far from it; only ye see my boy could not *pass his luck;* so that it's only natural for me to watch and see how he's trated.' Any interference in married feuds is dangerous, and in this particularly so; an observer will generally find that the mother-in-law takes the part of the son-in-law, and the husband's mother of her own son.

MRS S. C. HALL, *Ireland*, 1841

GOD'S CHURCH

Celtic cross

Les Irlandois naturels sont généralement Papistes, et fort attachés à la
Religion Romaine, peut-être plus par aversion pour les Anglois que par
bonnes raisons.

J. BEEVERELL, *Les Délices de la Grande Bretagne et de l'Irlande*, 1727

For several centuries in Ireland a Protestant (and English-speaking) minority used the apparatus of state to crush the Catholic
(and Irish-speaking) majority. Theology aside therefore, it is
scarcely to be wondered at that the mass of the people rejected
'Luther's Bible and his false black teaching', to borrow the words
of an 18th-century Irish poet: such terms are common in Irish literature throughout this period. Another poet, Owen Roe O'Sullivan
(1748–84), describes English Protestants as 'the dregs of Calvin-

ists', 'the vicious gang of Luther'. On the other hand, as if to sum up the faith of the Catholic Irish in 'their' church, he uses the term *Eaglais Dé*: God's Church.

The Catholicism of the Irish, like that of the Poles but unlike that of the Italians or French, was dearly bought and therefore all the more to be cherished. But if the Irish were loyal to their faith, they were not mindless sheep. Or rather, as Dr. S. J. Connolly has shown in a recent book,* they were happy to follow their shepherds provided they took them where the sheep wanted to go. Of their attendance at Sunday mass, for example, which in recent decades has been more than ninety per cent, he says 'it is difficult to believe that [it] can have greatly exceeded forty per cent of total Catholic numbers'.

Dr Connolly presents a revealing comparison between Irish- and English-speaking areas, using statistics from the 1850s and 1860s. Mass attendance, he suggests, was lower in Irish-speaking areas, and sometimes as low as twenty per cent, whereas the rate of illegitimate births was also lower in these areas. In his words, 'The pattern of Irish chastity appears to have run quite counter to that of Irish Catholic piety.' He links the legendary chastity of the Irish to the 'social and economic importance of the family in pre-famine Ireland'. The Irish had, he says, 'a great feeling against bastards' not only because they put a strain on the fragile family economy, but also because of the older notions of ancestry and status. He concludes his treatment of this question by stating:

Where discussions centered on the twentieth century have frequently seen the priest as the principal force behind the obsessive chastity of the Irish, a longer perspective suggests that his true role was rather to articulate and reinforce an outlook whose roots lay far deeper in the structure and assumptions of the society of which he was himself a product.

The Church won the chastity battle, says Dr Connolly in sub-

---

* Connolly (*op.cit.*), pp. 88-89, 215-218.

stance, because it was preaching to the converted. But when its message conflicted with the values of Gaelic society – when it tried to stop brawling and drunkenness, for example, or the hanky-hanky at wakes, all of which he studies in detail – it had nowhere near as much success.

Mass Is Secretly Said

In truth the Irish are naturally inclined to the Catholic religion; there are even in Dublin more than twenty houses where mass is secretly said, and above a thousand places, and subterraneous vaults and retired spots in the woods, where the peasants assemble to hear mass celebrated by some priests they secretly maintain. I consider it as a fact that one third of the Irish are Catholics, wherefore if any Catholic prince was to attempt the conquest of Ireland, I believe he would be readily seconded by the inhabitants. On this account perhaps it is that there are garrisons in all

At Mass

maritime places, and the entries and ports are always guarded . . .

I was in [Drogheda] on a Sunday, and was told that if I was desirous of hearing mass, one would be said at two miles distance from the town. It would be astonishing to relate the numbers of Catholics that I saw arrive from across the woods and mountains to assemble at this mass, which was said in a little hamlet, and in a chamber poorly fitted up. Here I saw, before mass, above fifty persons confess, and afterwards communicate with a devotion truly Catholic, and sufficient to draw these blind religionists to the true faith. The chapel in which the priest celebrated mass was not better adorned than the chamber; but God does not seek grand palaces, He chooses poverty and pureness of heart in those that serve Him. This priest informed me that the Irish were naturally inclined to the Catholic faith, but that there were many in different parts of the kingdom who found great difficulty to perform freely the functions of their religion. He had studied long in France, and spoke the French language well. He told me the Irish Catholics did not eat either flesh or eggs on Wednesdays, Fridays, or Saturdays; that they followed the commandments of the Church, and of our holy Father the Pope, whom they acknowledged for chief of the Catholic, Apostolic and Roman Church. This good man discoursed with me touching many difficulties there were in exercising the Catholic religion among the Protestants.

ALBERT JOUVIN DE ROCHEFORT, *Ireland Under The Restoration*, 1667

On Christmas Day
The Yeare 1678

Luke Waddinge, Coadjutor Bishop of Ferns (Wexford), wrote this song 'when the clergie were banished in the time of the plot', that is the Titus Oates plot of 1678, as a result of which many priests and bishops had to leave Ireland.

This is our Christmas day
The day of Christs birth
Yet we are far from Joy
And far from Christmass mirth
On Christmass to have no masse
Is our great discontent
That with out mass this day should pass
Doth cause us to lament.

The name of Christmass
Must chang'd and altered be
For since we have noe Masse
No Christmasse have we
It's therefore we do mourne
With grief our hearts Are prest
With tears our Eyes doe Run
Our minds and thoughts want rest.

As Jeremie sadly sate
With teares for to lament
The temple desolate
Her gould and glory spent
Soe we doe greive and mourne
To see no Priest at masse
No light on Alters burn
This day of Christmasse.

Christmas Candle

No masse heard this great day
No mattins sung last night
No bells to call to pray
No lamps, no taper light
No chalice, no rich robes
No Church no Chapple drest
No Vestments precious Coapes
No holy water blest.

Kind David in his dayes
Before the Arke did dance
With musicke and with praise
Its honour to Advance
But we our sad Eyes fix
To see layd on the ground
Our Arke our Crucifix
Our tabernacle downe.

Our Pictures daily open
As bookes before our Eyes
To read what we hear spoaken
Of Sacred misteries
They now are laid asside
And cast out of their place
Themselves from us they hide
In darkness and disgrace.

But if Church wales could speak
And Old times to us tell
If dead those graves could breake
Where thousand years they dwell
If that they could Arise
To preach what practis'd was
We should have Preists always
Our Aulters and our Masse.

Most pure and precious things
Were given in those times
By Emperours, Queens and Kings
With gould and silver shrines
They deem'd nothing too rich
That through their hands could pass
To beautify the Church
And to set forth the Masse.

What those first Christians left us
Written by their pen
What learned fathers taught us
Great saints and holy men
What in their times was done
And practis'd in each place
As Cleare as shines the sun
Doth show they still had Masse.

But good Old times are past
And new bad times are come
And worser times make hast
And hasten to us soone
Therfore in frights and feares
Those holy-dayes we pass
In sorrow and in teares
We spend our Christmass.

Some news each post doth bring
Of Jesuits and their plots
Against our sacred King
Discovered first by Oates
Such plotters we may Curss
With bell and booke at masse
By them the time is worse
Than 'ere we felt it was.

God bless our King and Queene
Long may they live in peace
Long may their dayes be seen
Long may their Joyes increase
And those that doe not pray
That Charles in peace may raigne
I wish they never may
See Priest nor Masse again.

LUKE WADDINGE, 1678

Hunting for Priests

An Exchange of Letters between Officials

To Capt. William Barton one of her Maiesties Justices of the peace at Thomastown neare Dundalk.

Dublin Castle 25 October 1712.

Sir,

   The Lords Justices and Council having received an Information that the titular popish Primate McMahon is lately come into this kingdom from Flanders and now resides at the house of Cullogh Duff McMahon near Carrickmacross their Excellencies and Lordships have commanded me to acquaint you therewith and to desire you will immediately take such numbers of persons as you shall think necessary and proper for that service and cause the said Primate to be apprehended and committed to Gaole and his papers to be sealed upp and sent to the Council Board and that you will give their Excellencies and Lordships an account of your proceedings therein

I am, Sir, Your most humble servant,

J. DAWSON.

William Barton's reply:

Thomastown October 30 1712.

Sir,

   I was favoured with your letter of the 25th and pursuant thereto I went with a party and all secretly by moonlight to Cullogh Duff McMahon's house about three miles from Carrickmacross and diligently searched it and every out house and crate [creaght – cattle byre] near it but met with no such like person as you write of and only three or four poor labourers and some women and Cullagh Duff on a straw bed with napy blankets and sacks stuffed with straw for a Bolster who reddily got up and with lights we looked in every place for papers under the pretence for stolen goods that we heard were brought thither and I believe they will think that was the occasion of our going thither and if the person you mention did ever lye there he would have some more decensy of a lodging than any was there. Of which pray inform their Excellencies and Lordships

> from Sir your most humble servant,
> WILLIAM BARTON

Epitaph

Epitaph said to have been carved on the back of the tombstone of a notorious priest-catcher:

> God is pleased when man doth cease to sin
> The devil is pleased when he a soul doth win
> Mankind are pleased whene'er a villain dies
> Now all are pleased for here Jack Cusack lies.

From a Letter to Rome

When our priests were confronted with greater dangers and were mercilessly pursued by government, some in order to prevent being identified by any in the congregation celebrated mass with veiled faces, others again shut themselves into a closet with the mass server alone and apertures were made or a small hole by means of which the people outside could hear the voice of the celebrant but could not recognise it, or at all events could not see him. And the mercy of God was only manifested the more, for as the persecution increased the fervour of the people increased also. Not uncommonly one would come across men and women with their hands joined in prayer – having got the signal that mass was begun – and thus they united themselves in spirit with those who afar off were praying on bended knee although they could not see the priest. It often happened to myself when saying mass by night that not a soul was present except the man of the house and his wife – not even the children for they could not be trusted with the secret. There was a penalty of £30 and a year's imprisonment on any who permitted mass to be said in his house or anywhere on his premises . . .

DR HUGH MACMAHON, Primate of Ireland, early 18th century

Exciting Christ's Sheep

Little Irish prose was written, and even less published, in the 18th century. In 1736, 'with no other view than to rescue Christ's sheep from the lion's jaw by reclaiming them from vice, and exciting them to virtue', the Bishop of Raphoe, James Gallager, published a book of sermons whose lively style made them very popular. In the Introduction, which he wrote in English, he explained why he had avoided the old literary language.

I have made them in an easy and familiar style, and on purpose omitted cramp expressions which might be obscure to both the preacher and hearer. Nay, instead of such, I have sometimes made use of words borrowed from the English, which practice and daily conversation have intermixed with our language, choosing with St. Augustine rather to be censured by the critics than not to be understood by the poor and illiterate, for whose use I have designed them. *Malo ut me reprehendant grammatici quam non intelligant populi.*

If my brethren will admire why Irish sermons should come clothed in English dress which seems not to suit so well the Irish language, one reason is that our printers have no Irish types, and another that our mother language, sharing so far the fate of her professors, is so far abandoned and is so great a stranger in her native soil that scarce one in ten is acquainted with her characters. Lest any, then, should be discouraged from making use of this little work by being strangers to its very elements, I have made choice of letters which are obvious to all, and in spelling kept nearer to the present manner of speaking than to the true and ancient orthography. This seeming difficulty being removed, I hope that as many as can speak or tolerably pronounce the Irish, if furnished with any stock of zeal to discharge their duty, will with little pains soon read and understand the following discourses.

Take, then, cheerfully, beloved fellow-labourer, this small mess of which I make you a gift, with which you may feed your flock once a month through the year and have some to spare; nay, rather than they should fast, spare not to give them each Sunday a part of the loaf by preaching a point, or even a paragraph, for there are some by their length which can afford to be divided. And by the time your store is exhausted you will acquire a facility both of expression and invention to serve up fresh dishes of your own dressing.

JAMES GALLAGHER, *Sermons*, 1736

The Reason Why Mass Is Said in Latin

'The sentiments are *Catholic*, the devotion, which it inspires is *solid,* and the morality is *exact, pious*, and *profitable*.'

So ran the introduction of the bilingual *Catechism* which Andrew Donlevy published in Paris in 1742. Like Gallagher's *Sermons*, this was one of the few printed books in their own language to circulate among the peasantry. In this extract the words are English, the subject is Latin, but the syntax and cadence are unmistakeably Irish.

Q. Is it not hurtful to the people that the Mass should be celebrated in a language which is not understood by all of them?
A. It is not: for the Mass is only a Prayer and a Sacrifice, which the priest alone is obliged to offer for the people. Moreover, the Church commands every parish priest to expound often some part of the Mass to the People; or to get it expounded for them, and particularly on Sundays and Holy-Days.

Again, it is manifest, although the Latin be a dead language, that there is no language in Europe more universally understood; there being scarcely a village without somebody that understands it: so that it cannot truly be said that it is an unknown tongue.

Q. Why does the Church make use of the Latin in preference to any other language in Europe?

A. First, it is more universally understood than any other language. In the next place, because it is a dead language, not subject to change, it is in it the Liturgy or Common Prayers of the Church can best be preserved from alteration and corruption: a thing which could hardly be done if the Mass were turned into all the different and variable jargons, spoken not only in each country, but also in many provinces and remote districts of almost each district throughout all Europe.

Besides that it is a great comfort to travellers and foreigners to find the public prayers of the Church *uniform* or the very same, both at home and abroad; so that they must indeed be very idiots, if they know not when to say Amen, when to kneel, when to stand, or do any thing that concerns them, or that is proper for them to do.

ANDREW DONLEVY, Catechism, 1742

Timoleague

Timoleague Abbey in Co. Cork was burned by the English in 1642.

One night I walked by the sea shore and came to the ruins of the great Abbey of Timoleague. With a heavy heart I made this sad lament:

> O, empty roofless ruin
> Dwelling house and tower,
> Many stormy winds

Have beaten on your walls,
Much rain and cold
And sea-gales you withstood
Since you were offered first
As shelter for Our Lord.

Jagged walls mossed with grass
Once a glory to this country,
I grieve for your fall
And your holy men sent wandering,
Here now is loneliness
No harmony within
The harsh screech of the owl
In place of chanted hymns.

Ivy creeps on your arches
Red nettles matt the floor
The rangy fox whines thinly
In crannies mumble stoats,
Where the skylark sang out early
To friars chanting hours,
No clear sound now of tongues,
But the jabbering of daws.
No meat in your dining rooms
No sun-bleached beds aloft,
All that whiten in your shelter now
Are honeycombs of bones,
Your nuns and Franciscans
Left you in great sorrow,
Your glebe without ceremony
Or a mass being said to God.

Attack and foreign cruelty
Base tyranny and malice
Strong arms and gross looting

Left you lonely as you are;
I, too, prospered once
But my character declined,
The world came against me
I am vigorless and blind,
My face is a twisted mask,
My heart a fruitless husk,
My friends lie in this graveyard
To turn reluctant dust –
If Death comes
I'll welcome him.

SEÁN Ó COILEÁIN (c.1754-1817)
Trans. JOAN KEEFE

Ruins of Jerpoint Abbey (Co. Kilkenny)

Eloquence

The eloquence of a country priest, though rude, and by no means elevated, is sometimes well adapted to the end in view, to the feelings of his auditory, and to the nature of the subject on which he speaks. Pathos and humour are the two levers by which the Irish character is raised or depressed; and these are blended in a manner too anomalous to be ever properly described. Whoever could be present at a sermon on the Sunday when a Purgatorian Society is to be established, would hear pathos and see grief of the first water. It is then he would get a 'nate' and glowing description of Purgatory, and see the broad, humorous, Milesian faces, of three or four thousand persons of both sexes, shaped into an expression of the most grotesque and clamorous grief. The priest however, on particular occasions of this nature, very shrewdly gives notice of the sermon, and of the purpose for which it is to be preached; – if it be grave, the people are prepared to cry; but if it be for a political, or any other purpose not decidedly religious, there will be abundance of that rough, blunt satire and mirth, so keenly relished by the peasantry, illustrated, too, by the most comical and ridiculous allusions. That priest, indeed, who is the best master of this latter faculty is uniformly the greatest favourite. It is no unfrequent thing to see the majority of an Irish congregation drowned in sorrow and tears, even when they are utterly ignorant of the language spoken; particularly in those districts where the Irish is still the vernacular tongue. This is what renders notice of the sermon and its purport necessary; otherwise the honest people might be seriously at a loss whether to laugh or cry.

'*Ellish, avourneen, gho dhe dirsha?*' – Ellish, my dear, what is he saying?'

'*Och, musha niel eshighum, ahagur – ta sha er Purgathor, ta barrllium,*' – Och, I dunna that, jewel; I blieve he's on Purgatory.'

'Och, och, oh – och, och, oh – oh, i, oh, i, oh!'

And on understanding that Purgatory is the subject, they commence their grief with a rocking motion, wringing their hands, and unconsciously passing their beads through their fingers, whilst their bodies are bent forward.

WILLIAM CARLETON, *Traits and Stories of the Irish Peasantry,* 1830–33

The Future Priest

The highest object of an Irish peasant's ambition is to see his son a priest. Whenever a farmer happens to have a large family, he usually destines one of them for the church, if his circumstances are at all such as can enable him to afford the boy a proper education. This youth becomes the centre in which all the affections of the family meet. He is cherished, humoured in all his caprices, indulged in his boyish predilections, and raised over the heads of his brothers, independently of all personal or relative merit in himself. The consequence is, that he gradually becomes self-willed, proud, and arrogant, often to an offensive degree; but all this is frequently mixed up with a lofty bombast, and an undercurrent of strong disguised affection, that render his early life remarkably ludicrous and amusing. Indeed, the pranks of pedantry, the pretensions to knowledge, and the humour with which it is mostly displayed, render these scions of divinity, in their intercourse with the people until the period of preparatory education is completed, the most interesting and comical class, perhaps, to be found in the kingdom.

WILLIAM CARLETON, *Traits and Stories of the Irish Peasantry,* 1830–33

Cahir's Catholic Chapel

One of the vexations of the Penal Laws was that Irish Catholics had to make do with simple mass-houses or chapels in obscure streets. As their position improved, however, and especially after the passing of the Catholic Emancipation Act in 1829, they set about building bigger and better churches, eager to outdo the Protestants.

As this Tale of Two Churches reminds us, it is difficult to build without getting dirt on your hands.

Tuam Cathedral in the early 1840s

The town of Cahir lies on the side of a hill; and is adorned by two very pretty spires; one, belonging to the new Protestant church, a handsome little edifice; the other, appertaining to the Catholic chapel, a grander and far larger edifice. A considerable number of the most recently erected Catholic chapels have spires, which, in height and architecture, quite eclipse those of the churches of the Establishment.

I am sorry to be obliged, in this place, to record a fact, to which I could not have given credit on any evidence, less conclusive than that of my own eyes. The Roman Catholic chapel is newly erected, and is yet unfinished: and I was told, that the anxiety to obtain funds for its completion, gave rise to the enaction of some curious scenes at the door. I went there, about ten o'clock; and I certainly did witness a scene of a most singular kind. The gates were shut, and four men stood by. One had a silver salver, to receive the larger contributions: two were provided with wooden ladles, for the copper offerings; and these they shook in the ears of every one who approached: and one man, the priest, stood, just within the gate, armed with a shillelah. *No one was admitted who did not contribute!* I saw a man attempt to pass without contributing; and I saw the priest push and buffet the man, and, at length, strike him several times with his stick, and knock his hat off his head! This is no matter of hearsay. I saw it: and I saw from thirty to forty persons kneeling outside of the gate, on the high road, – poor persons, who had not a halfpenny to spare. To be more and more sure, that this was the cause of their remaining without, I gave some halfpence amongst them, and saw them admitted.

HENRY D. INGLIS, *Journeys Throughout Ireland,* 1834

The Sister of Charity

She once was a lady of honour and wealth,
Bright glowed on her features the roses of health,
Her vesture was blended of silk and of gold,
And her motion shook perfume from every fold;
Joy revelled around her – love shone at her side,
And gay was her smile, as the glance of a bride;
And light was her step in the mirth-sounding hall,
When she heard of the daughters of Vincent de Paul.

She felt in her spirit the summons of grace,
That called her to live for the suffering race,
And, heedless of pleasure, of comfort, of home,
Rose quickly, like Mary, and answered: 'I come!'
She put from her person the trappings of pride,
And passed from her home with the joy of a bride;
Nor wept at the threshold, as onward she moved,
For her heart was on fire in the cause it approved.

Lost ever to fashion – to vanity lost,
That beauty that once was the song and the toast,
No more in the ball-room that figure we meet,
But, gliding at dusk to the wretch's retreat.

Forgot in the halls is that high-sounding name,
For the Sister of Charity blushes at fame;
Forgot all the claims of her riches and birth,
For she barters for Heaven the glory of earth.

Those feet that to music could gracefully move
Now bear her alone on the mission of love;
Those hands that once dangled the perfume and gem
Are tending the helpless, or lifted for them;
That voice that once echoed the song of the vain
Now whispers relief to the bosom of pain,
And the hair that was shining with diamond and pearl
Is wet with the tears of the penitent girl.

Her down-bed a pallet – her trinkets a bead,
Her lustre – one taper that serves her to read;
Her sculpture – the crucifix nailed by her bed,
Her paintings – one print of the thorn-crowned head;
Her cushion – the pavement that wearies her knees,
Her music – the Psalm, or the sigh of disease;
The delicate lady lives mortified there,
And the feast is forsaken for fasting and prayer.

Yet not to the service of heart and of mind,
Are the cares of that Heaven-minded virgin confined;
Like Him whom she loves, to the mansions of grief
She hastes with the tidings of joy and relief.
She strengthens the weary – she comforts the weak,
And soft is her voice in the ear of the sick;
Where want and affliction on mortals attend,
The Sister of Charity there is a friend.

Unshrinking where pestilence scatters his breath,
Like an angel she moves,'mid the vapour of death;
Where rings the loud musket, and flashes the sword,
Unfearing she walks, for she follows the Lord.

How sweetly she bends o'er each plague-tainted face
With looks that are lighted with holiest grace;
How kindly she dresses each suffering limb,
For she sees in the wounded the image of Him.

Behold her, ye worldly! behold her, ye vain!
Who shrink from the pathway of virtue and pain;
Who yield up to pleasure your nights and your days,
Forgetful of service, forgetful of praise.
Ye lazy philosophers – self-seeking men –
Ye fireside philantrophists, great at the pen;
How stands in the balance your eloquence weighed
With the life and the deeds of that high-born maid?

GERALD GRIFFIN (1803–1840)

Thackeray in Ireland

The popular and resurgent Catholicism which William Makepeace Thackeray saw when he visited Ireland a few years before
the Famine both fascinated and dismayed him. His impressions
are of interest not only for what they tell of religious practice at
the time, but also for what they disclose of his own prejudices.

Sunday Morning in Skibbereen

The people came flocking into the place by hundreds, and you saw
their blue cloaks dotting the road and the bare open plains beyond.
The men came with shoes and stockings today, the women all bare-
legged, and many of them might be seen washing their feet in the
stream before they went up to the chapel. The street seemed to be
lined on either side with blue cloaks, squatting along the doorways
as is their wont. Among these, numberless cows were walking to
and fro, and pails of milk passing, and here and there a hound or two
went stalking about ... Anybody at eight o'clock of a Sunday
morning in summer may behold the above scene from a bridge just
above the town. He may add to it the river, with one or two barges

Inhabitants of Connemara on the way to Mass.
The man in front carries his shoes to avoid wearing
them out unnecessarily.

lying idle upon it; a flag flying at what looks like a custom-house; bare country all around; and the chapel before him, with a swarm of the dark figures round about it.

I went into it, not without awe, (for ... I always feel a sort of tremor on going into a Catholic place of worship: the candles, and altars, and mysteries, the priest and his robes, and nasal chaunting, and wonderful genuflexions, will frighten me as long as I live). The chapel-yard was filled with men and women: a couple of shabby old beadles were at the gate, with copper shovels to collect money; and inside the chapel four or five hundred people were on their knees, and scores more of the blue-mantles came in, dropping their curtsies as they entered, and then taking their places on the flags.

Assumption Day in Tralee

The most curious sight of the town was the chapel, with the festival held there. It was the feast of the Assumption of the Virgin, (let those who are acquainted with the calendar and the facts it commemorates say what the feast was, and when it falls), and all the country seemed to be present on the occasion: the chapel and the large court leading to it were thronged with worshippers, such as one never sees in our country, where devotion is by no means so crowded as here. Here, in the court-yard, there were thousands of them on their knees, rosary in hand, for the most part praying, and mumbling, and casting a wistful look round as the strangers passed. In a corner was an old man groaning in the agonies of death or colic, and a woman got off her knees to ask us for charity for the unhappy old fellow. In the chapel the crowd was enormous: the priest and his people were kneeling, and bowing, and humming, and chanting, and censer-rattling; the ghostly crew being attended by a fellow that I don't remember to have seen in continental churches, a sort of Catholic clerk, a black shadow to the parson, bowing his head when his reverence bowed, kneeling when he knelt, only three steps lower.

But we who wonder at copes and candlesticks, see nothing strange in surplices and beadles. A Turk, doubtless, would sneer equally at each, and have you to understand that the only reasonable ceremonial was that which took place at his mosque.

Whether right or wrong in point of ceremony, it was evident the heart of devotion was there: the immense crowd moaned and swayed, and you heard a hum of all sorts of wild ejaculations, each man praying seemingly for himself, while the service went on at the altar. The altar candles flickered red in the dark, steaming place, and every now and then from the choir you heard a sweet female voice chanting Mozart's music, which swept over the heads of the people a great deal more pure and delicious than the best incense that ever smoked out of the pot.

On the chapel-floor, just at the entry, lay several people moaning, and tossing, and telling their beads. Behind the old woman was a font of holy water, up to which little children were clambering; and in the chapel-yard were several old women . . . with tin cans full of the same sacred fluid, with which the people, as they entered, aspersed themselves with all their might, flicking a great quantity into their faces, and making a curtsey and a prayer at the same time . . .

When I came out of the chapel, the old fellow on the point of death was still howling and groaning in so vehement a manner, that I heartily trust he was an imposter, and that on receiving a sixpence he went home tolerably comfortable, having secured a maintenance for that day. But it will be long before I can forget the strange, wild scene, so entirely different was it from the decent and comfortable observances of our own Church.

Visit to a Nunnery

We were shown into a gay parlour [in the Ursuline Convent, Blackrock, Co. Cork], and presently Sister Two-Eight made her appearance – a pretty and graceful lady, attired as on this page. . .

Sister Two-Eight

I must own that slim, gentle and pretty as the young lady was, and calculated with her kind smiling face and little figure to frighten no one in the world, a great six-foot Protestant could not help looking at her with a little tremble. I had never been in a nun's company before; I'm afraid of such – I don't care to own – in their black mysterious robes and awful veils. As priests in gorgeous vestments, and little rosy incense-boys in red, bob their heads and knees up and down before altars, or clatter silver pots full of smoking odours I feel I don't know what sort of thrill and secret creeping terror. Here I was, in a room with a real live nun, pretty and pale – I wonder has she any of her sisterhood immured in *oubliettes* down below; is her poor little weak, delicate body scarred all over with scourgings, iron-collars, hair-shirts? What has she had for dinner today? – as we passed the refectory there was a faint sort of vapid nun-like vegetable smell, speaking of fasts and wooden platters; and I could picture to myself silent sisters eating their meal – a grim old yellow one in the reading desk, croaking out an extract from a sermon for their edification . . .

Were all the smiles of that kind-looking Sister Two-Eight perfectly sincere? Whenever she spoke her face was lighted up with one. She seemed perfectly radiant with happiness, tripping lightly before us, and distributing kind compliments to each, which made me in a very few minutes forget the introductory fright which her poor little presence had occasioned.

She took us through the hall (where there was the vegetable savour before mentioned) and showed us the contrivance by which the name of Two-Eight was ascertained. Each nun has a number, or combination of numbers, prefixed to her name; and a bell is pulled a corresponding number of times, by which each sister knows when she is wanted. Poor souls! are they always on the look-out for that bell, that the ringing of it should be supposed infallibly to awaken their attention? . . .

We were taken through a hall decorated with a series of pictures of Pope Pius VI [until] ... we came into a long, clean, lofty passage, with many little doors on each side; and here I confess my heart began to thump again. These were the doors of the cells of the Sisters. *Bon Dieu*! and is it possible that I shall see a nun's cell? Do I not recollect the nun's cell in 'The Monk', or in 'The Romance of the Forest?' or, if not there, at any rate, in a thousand noble romances, read in early days of half-holiday perhaps – romances at twopence a volume.

Come in, in the name of the saints! Here is the cell. I took off my hat and examined the little room with much curious wonder and reverence. There was an iron bed, with comfortable curtains of green serge. There was a little clothes-chest of yellow wood, neatly cleaned, and a wooden chair beside it, and a desk on the chest, and about six pictures on the wall – little religious pictures: a saint with gilt paper round him; the Virgin showing on her breast a bleeding heart, with a sword run through it; and other sad little objects, calculated to make the inmates of the cell think of the saints and martyrs of the Church. Then there was a little crucifix, and a wax-candle on the ledge; and here was the place where the poor black-veiled things were to pass their lives for ever!

After having seen a couple of these little cells, we left the corridors in which they were, and were conducted, with a sort of pride on the nun's part, I thought, into the grand room of the convent – a parlour with pictures of saints, and a gay paper, and a series of small fineries, such only as women very idle know how to make. There were some portraits in the room, one an atrocious daub of an ugly old woman, surrounded by children still more hideous...

And now we had seen all the wonders of the house but the chapel, and thither we were conducted; all the ladies of our party kneeling down as they entered the building, and saying a short prayer.

This, as I am on sentimental confessions, I must own affected me too. It was a very pretty and tender sight. I should have liked to kneel down too, but was ashamed; our northern usages not encouraging – among men at least – that sort of abandonment of dignity. Do any of us dare to sing psalms at church? and don't we look with rather a sneer at a man who does?

The chapel had nothing remarkable in it except a very good organ, as I was told; for we were allowed only to see the exterior of that instrument, our pious guide with much pleasure removing an oil-cloth which covered the mahogany. At one side of the altar is a long high *grille,* through which you see a hall, where the nuns have their stalls, and sit in chapel time; and beyond this hall is another small chapel, with a couple of altars, and one beautiful print in one of them – a German Holy Family – a prim, mystical, tender piece, just befitting the place.

In the *grille* is a little wicket and a ledge before it. It is to this wicket that women are brought to kneel; and a bishop is in the chapel on the other side, and takes their hands in his, and receives their vows. I had never seen the like before, and own that I felt a sort of shudder at looking at the place. There rest the girl's knees as she offers herself up, and foreswears the sacred affections which God gave her; there she kneels and denies forever the beautiful duties of her being: – no tender maternal yearnings, no gentle attachments are to be had for her or from her – there she kneels and commits suicide upon her heart. O honest Martin Luther! thank God, you came down to pull that infernal, wicked, unnatural altar down – that cursed Paganism! Let people solitary, worn-out by sorrow or oppressed by extreme remorse, retire to such places; fly and beat your breasts in caverns and wildernesses, O women, if you will, but be Magdalens first. It is shameful that any young girl, with any vocation however seemingly strong, should be allowed to bury herself in this small tomb of a few acres. Look at yonder nun, – pretty, smiling, graceful, and young, – what has God's world done to *her,* that she should run from it, or she done to the world, that she should avoid it? What call has she to give up all her duties and affections? and would she not be best serving God with a husband at her side, and a child on her knee?

WILLIAM MAKEPEACE THACKERAY, *The Irish Sketch Book*, 1843

High Mass in Dublin

A German tourist sees the Irish at prayer.

The divine service here was more sacred and more solemn than I had observed it elsewhere. It was simple – the singing of the high mass was not indifferent – but that which gave the peculiar character of solemnity to the entire, was the conduct, the bearing of the congregation . . . In Germany one may be seen leaning against a pillar in the church, another lolling on the bench – in Paris the grand dames and opera ladies repose on satin-covered stools, and the dandies stand and greet them in the aisles; but in Dublin there prevails the strictest, the most uniform discipline. All are attentive to the bell, and when its first tinkling sounds are heard, every knee, without distinction, bends in reverence, whether it rests upon a wooden flooring, a carpetted board, or the hard stone. There was piety, there was true religion in the looks of all, and I could not but think of the early days of my boyhood, when the ardour of faith filled my breast also, and hours of holiness were passed by me in the Cathedral of Cologne. The people around me prayed aloud – so loudly, that I could hear distinctly what they said in their prayers on my right hand and on my left; and then, when it came to the most solemn part of the mass – when the consecration was completed, and the priest raised the sacrament in his hand – I could hear the poor people near me strike themselves on the breast with such force, that the blows re-echoed through the church.

J. VENEDEY, *Ireland and the Irish during the Repeal Year*, 1843

Prayers

A Health

A health let us drink. Our glass we clink it,
  May the King of the Graces to us be near.
We will drink this glass as Patrick would drink it,
  With a grace made salt by a mingled tear,
Without sadness or sorrow or passion or pain,
  – None knowing tomorrow that we were here.

O Mary of Graces

O Mary of Graces
  And Mother of God,
May I tread in the paths
  That the righteous have trod.

And mayest thou save me
  From Evil's control,
And mayest thou save me
  In body and soul.

And mayest thou save me
  By land and by sea,
And mayest thou save me
  From tortures to be.

May the guard of the angels
  Above me abide,
May God be before me
  And God at my side.

Traditional
Trans. DOUGLAS HYDE

Entertaining the parish priest and his curate

Is Nothing Sacred?

A Difficult Parishioner

These two anecdotes are told of Anthony Raftery the poet.

There was a man in Crostachan, near Loughrea, and two hundred heads of cabbage were stolen from him one night. The priest spoke from the altar about this ugly business, saying how it was a great scandal. As he was speaking he observed that Raftery was in the congregation, and he asked: 'What do you say, Raftery, of the man who stole the cabbage?'

Raftery, who thought that the priest was making too much of a small affair of the kind, cried out: –

> Father, I say,
> He who ate two hundred heads of cabbage,
> That great was his courage!
> If they had been boiled with meat

> Sure they would satisfy the parish!
> Since it is you, father, who have spent
> So long in college,
> Did you ever read
> That much about cabbage?

He was going to add more to this when the priest stopped him.

There was another priest, one day, who was teaching him how to baptise a child, for there were houses scattered about in that country far from any priest, and certain people had the right to baptise children if in danger of death. The priest placed an old worn-out hat in Raftery's hand, as though it were a child that was on it, and taught him the words he had to say. But what Raftery said was:—

> I baptise thee, my child, without bottom or top,
> Without water or salt, or of whiskey one drop,
> The three waves baptismal I pour on thy top;
> A ram was thy father, a sheep was thy mother,
> And I never am like to baptise such another.

Attributed to ANTHONY RAFTERY (1784–1835)
Trans. DOUGLAS HYDE

Flesh and Blood

As Merriman reminds us in his 18th-century satire *The Midnight Court*, celibacy was a problem not only for young curates, but also for the women in their congregation, who often found them a source of temptation.

> What is the use of the rule insane
> That marriage has closed to the clerical clan
> In the church of our fathers since first it began.
> It's a melancholy sight to a needy maid
> Their comely faces and forms displayed,
> Their hips and thighs so broad and round,
> Their buttocks and breasts that in flesh abound,
> Their lustrous looks and their lusty limbs,
> Their fair fresh features, their smooth soft skins,

Their strength and stature, their force and fire,
Their craving curbed and uncooled desire.
They eat and drink of the fat of the land,
They've wealth and comfort at their command,
They sleep on beds of the softest down,
They've ease and leisure their lot to crown,
They commence in manhood's prime and flood,
And well we know that they're flesh and blood!
If I thought that sexless saints they were
Or holy angels, I would not care,
But they're lusty lads with a crave unsated
In slothful sleep, and the maids unmated.
We know it is true there are few but hate
The lonely life and the celibate state;
Is it fair to condemn them to mope and moan,
Is it fair to force them to lie alone,
To bereave of issue a sturdy band
The fruit of whose loins might free the land?
Tho' some of them ever were grim and gruff,
Intractable, sullen and stern and tough,
Crabbed and cross, unkind and cold,
Surly and wont to scowl and scold,
Many are made of warmer clay,
Affectionate, ardent, kind and gay;
It's often a woman got land or wealth,
Store or stock from a priest by stealth,
Many's the case I call to mind
Of clergymen who were slyly kind,
I could show you women who were their flames,
And their children reared beneath false names;
And often I must lament in vain
How they waste their strength on the old and plain
While marriageable maids their plight deplore
Waiting unwooed thro' this senseless law;

'Tis a baleful ban to our hapless race
And beneath its sway we decay apace.
BRIAN MERRIMAN (1749–1805), *The Midnight Court*
Trans. ARLAND USSHER

Dukeen's Death

This brief elegy was written by the poet Egan O'Rahilly to commemorate an incident which took place in his own house. He had a
visitor one day, the steward of a local gentleman, known to the
people as *Stewardeen* (Little Steward). The steward had a
puppy called *Dukeen* (Little Duke), a keen and lively little dog.

The parish priest came to the house that same day, and at the
moment he was coming through the doorway, Dukeen leapt up
and seized him by the heel. What did the priest do but grab
Dukeen by the hind-legs and strike his head on the threshold, killing him.

> Alas! Dukeen
> will wait no more
> for Stewardeen
> at chapel-door.
> For he who rushed
> to seize a bone
> now lies here crushed
> on threshold-stone.
> Be gladdened by
> one thought at least:
> he did not die
> without a priest!

EGAN O'RAHILLY (c. 1675–1729)
Trans. FRANK MURPHY

HOLY DAYS AND HOLIDAYS

Dancers at a fair

For most people the only change from the drudgery of daily life came on Sundays and feast days. As the Irish language sources tell us little about how they spent these days, or their leisure moments in general, most of what we know comes from observations made by travellers and popular writers, especially in the first half of the 19th century.

Holy Days

These are the days on which there is a binding obligation to hear Mass, and to refrain from manual labour, namely:

> Every Sunday of the year.
> Christmas Day.

Feast of the Circumcision of the Lord.
Feast of the Epiphany.
St. Patrick's Day.
Feast of the Annunciation.
Ascension Thursday.
Feast of Corpus Christi.
Feast of Saints Peter and Paul.
Feast of the Assumption.
All Saints' Day.

REV. JONATHAN FURLONG, *Irish Prayer Book*, 1842
Trans. FRANK MURPHY

Christmas

Christmas-day passed among the peasantry, as it usually passes in Ireland. Friends met before dinner in their own, in their neigh-bours', in shebeen or in public houses, where they drank, sang, or fought, according to their natural dispositions, or the quantity of liquor they had taken. The festivity of the day might be known by the unusual reek of smoke that danced from each chimney, by the number of persons who crowded the roads, by their bran-new dresses, – for if a young man or country girl can afford a dress at all, they provide it for Christmas, – and by the striking appearance of those who, having drunk a little too much, were staggering home in the purest happiness, singing, stopping their friends, shaking hands with them, or kissing them, without any regard to sex. Many a time might be seen two Irishmen, who had got drunk together, leaving a fair or market, their arms about each other's necks, from whence they only removed them to kiss and hug one another the more lovingly. Notwithstanding this, there is nothing more probable than that these identical two will enjoy the luxury of a mutual bat-tle, by way of episode, and again proceed on their way, kissing and hugging as if nothing had happened to interrupt their friendship. All the usual effects of jollity and violence, fun and fighting, love and liquor, were, of course, to be seen felt, heard, and understood on this day, in a manner much more remarkable than on common occasions; for it may be observed, that the national festivals of the Irish bring out their strongest points of character with peculiar distinctness.

WILLIAM CARLETON *Traits and Stories of the Irish Peasantry*, 1830–33

Wren Day

Wren Day

The Wren-boys of Shanagolden, a small village in the southwest of Ireland, were all assembled pursuant to custom on the green before the chapel-door, on a fine frosty morning, being the twenty-sixth of December, or Saint Stephen's day – a festival yet held in much reverence in Munster, although the Catholic church has for many years ceased to look upon it as a holiday of 'obligation.' Seven or eight handsome young fellows, tricked out in ribands of the gayest colours, white waist-coats and stockings, and furnished with musical instruments of various kinds – a fife, a pipolo, an old drum, a cracked fiddle, and a set of bagpipes – assumed their place in the rear of the procession, and startled the yet slumbering inhabitants of the neighbouring houses, by a fearfully discordant prelude. Behind those came the Wren-boy, *par excellence*, a lad who bore in his hands a holly-bush, the leaves of which were interwoven with long streamers of red, yellow, blue, and white riband; all which finery, nevertheless, in no way contributed to reconcile the little mottled tenant of the bower (a wren which was tied by the leg to one of the boughs) to his state of durance. After the Wren-boy came a promiscuous crowd of youngsters, of all ages under fifteen, composing just such a little ragged rabble as one observes attending the band of a marching regiment on its entrance into a country town, shouting, hallooing, laughing, and joining in apt chorus with the droning, shrilling, squeaking, and rattling of the musicians of the morn.

GERALD GRIFFIN, *The Half-Sir*, 1829

Little Christmas

It was the eve of Little Christmas (New Year's Eve), and Poll Naughten was arranging at a small table the three-branched candle with which the vigil of this festival is celebrated in Catholic houses.

GERALD GRIFFIN, *The Collegians*, 1829

St Patrick's Eve

A multitude of people . . . were moving in confused and noisy procession along the street. An ancient and still honoured custom summons the youthful inhabitants of the city on the night of this anniversary to celebrate the approaching holiday of the patron saint and apostle of the island, by promenading all the streets in succession, playing national airs, and filling up the pauses in the music with shouts of exultation . . .

The appearance which [the procession] presented was not altogether destitute of interest and amusement. In the midst were a band of musicians who played alternately 'Patrick's Day' and 'Garryowen', while a rabble of men and boys pressed round them, thronging the whole breadth and a considerable portion of the length of the street. The men had got sprigs of shamrock in their hats, and several carried in their hand lighted candles, protected from the wasting night-blast by a simple lamp of whited brown paper. The fickle and unequal light which those small torches threw over the faces of the individuals who held them, afforded a lively contrast to the prevailing darkness.

The crowd hurried forward, singing, playing, shouting, laughing, and indulging, to its full extent, all the excitement which was occasioned by the tumult and the motion. Bedroom windows are thrown up as they passed, and the half dressed inmates thrust their heads into the night air to gaze upon the mob of enthusiasts. All the respectable persons who appeared in the streets as they advanced, turned short into the neighbouring byways to avoid the importunities which they would be likely to incur by a contact with the multitide.

GERALD GRIFFIN, *The Collegians*, 1829

Black Lent

Some of the lower orders of Roman catholics, who have been enjoined a strict fast (called by them *black Lent*), at the end of it, to show their exhilaration at its being over, carry about the streets an herring, which they whip with rods, to the great delight of all the blackguards and children of the place.

JOHN CARR, *The Stranger in Ireland*, 1805

Easter 1827

14th April The poor people are overjoyed at the thought that tomorrow they will have meat to eat. People are coming in to market from the country. Poor people in the country eat meat only three days a year, Christmas Day, Shrove Tuesday and Easter Sunday.

15th April Easter Sunday. Delightful day. At midday five of us left Callan to go to Desart Court... There is a beautiful view from this house. The breeze was soft, the hills to the south dark blue, Cnoc na Carraig immediately to the north covered by trees and Cnoc na Ratha to the northwest the same. The woods came round us, ash and oak... growing in the middle of evergreen pines, meadows as soft as silk or satin and as green as young corn. It's an earthly paradise. We went on to Butlers' and stopped for a meal of white bread, bacon, tasty mutton, 'speckled white pudding' and a drop of whiskey or barley juice to drink from the beautiful lady innkeeper. We went home merrily via Tullamore, Cnoc Riabhach, etc. The loveliest evening I ever saw.

16th April Easter Monday or Egg Day. Delightfully fine sunny morning. At midday, the young women and young men were eating their eggs and drinking in the taverns. In the evening, the taverns were still full of young people. Lovely day.

17th April 'The more you drink, the thirstier you become'... People were making a lot of noise in the streets at three o'clock in the morning, and they're still as drunk as ever. There's no mistaking them, these dirty bumpkins and bogtrotters and clod-hoppers without manners or education...

HUMPHREY O'SULLIVAN, *Diary*, 1827
Trans. FRANK MURPHY

May Day

To the Printer of the *Leinster Journal*

Sir,
For many years past the peace of this city [Kilkenny] has been disturbed every May-eve, by a vast multitude of audacious fel-

lows, who assemble together to collect May-balls among the new-married folks. They sally out with Herculanean clubs in their hands, and as those unmeaning May-balls are seldom or never given without a piece of drink-money to boot, such bloody battles ensue in different quarters of the town, such confusion and uproar, as would induce a passing stranger to believe that a furious band of wild Indians had broken in upon us; that Magistracy was asleep, or that it had lost all power and influence over the subject. The mischief that follows from this barbarous and unheeded custom is more feelingly understood than can be expressed. Not to mention the fractures, contusions, etc., which are well known to happen on such occasions, and by which many of those miscreants are disabled for a considerable time from working for themselves, and for the support of those who entirely depend upon their sound legs and arms, many Gentlemen's gardens are wantonly robbed of all their beauties, the cultivation of which cost the owner a vast deal of trouble and expense; the hedges and fences, in the outlets of our City, are stript of full-grown hawthorns, whose late blooming pride and fragrancy is now miserably dying away on dunghills before cabin doors, by way of May-bushes no longer, alas! to afford a nuptial bed to the newly married linnet and his mate, but fastened in the ground for the vilest purposes – To hang filthy clouts upon . . .

From a letter published in *Finn's Leinster Journal*, 4th May 1768

Pattern Day

Throughout Ireland are to be found many shrines and holy wells, which are often dedicated to local saints. The annual feast day to commemorate the patron saint of a given place was known as a pattern or patron day. Patterns were a curious blend of the sacred and the profane, and very popular, but the problems caused by their popularity sometimes brought them into bad odour with the clergy.

Praying at a pattern

St John

Gougaun Lake, or Lake Gouganebarra, is in West Cork.

My first visit to Gougaun Lake was on the 23d of June, 1813, the eve of St. John. Feeling a strong wish to be present at the celebration of an Irish patron, or religious meeting in remembrance of a particular saint – a mere boy at the time, I had toiled through a long and an arduous walk in company with one whose pen would more ably than mine have done justice to the scene . . .

After a walk of about seven Irish miles from the village of Inchegeela, we gained the brow of a mountain, and beheld the Lake of Gougaun with its little wooded island beneath us; one spot on its shore, swarming with people, appeared, from our elevated situation, to be a dark mass surrounded by moving specks, which continually merged into it. On our descent we caught the distant and indistinct murmur of the multitude; and as we approached and forded the eastern extremity of the lake, where its waters discharge themselves through a narrow and precipitous channel, an unseemly uproar burst upon us, though at a distance

of nearly half a mile from the assembly. It was not without difficulty that we forced our way through the crowd on the shore of
the lake, to the wall of the chapels on the island, where we stood
amid an immense concourse of people: the interior of the cells
were filled with men and women in various acts of devotion,
almost all of them on their knees; some, with hands uplifted,
prayed in loud voices, using considerable gesticulation, and
others, in a less noisy manner, rapidly counted the beads of their
rosary, or, as it is called by the Irish peasant, their pathereen, with
much apparent fervour; or, as a substitute for beads, threw from
one hand into the other, small pebbles to mark the number of
prayers they had repeated; whilst such of the men as were not
furnished with other means kept their reckoning by cutting a
notch on their cudgel, or on a piece of stick provided for the
purpose.

   To a piece of rusty iron, shaped thus, considerable importance
seems to have been attached; it passed from one devotee to
another with much ceremony. The form consisted in placing it
three times, with a short prayer, across the head of the nearest
person, to whom it was then handed, and who went through the
same ceremony with the next to him, and thus it circulated from
one to the other.

The crowd in the chapels every moment increasing, it became a matter of labour to force our way towards the shore, through the throng that covered the causeway. Adjoining the causeway, part of the water of the lake was inclosed and covered in as a well, by which name it was distinguished. On gaining the back of the well we observed a man, apparently of the mendicant order, describing, on a particular stone in its wall, the figure of a cross, with small pieces of slate, which he afterwards sold to such devotees as were desirous of possessing these relics.

The number of slates thus treated at various periods, had worn in the stone to which they were applied a cross nearly two inches in depth, and which every new sign served to deepen. The door or opening to the front of the well was so narrow as scarcely to admit two persons at the same time. Within, the well was crowded to excess, probably seven or eight persons, some with their arms, some with their legs thrust down into the water, exhibiting the most disgusting sores and shocking infirmities. When those within came out, their places were as instantly filled by others. Some there were who had waited two or three hours before they could obtain access to this 'healing fount.' The blind, the cripple, and the infirm jostled and retarded each other in their efforts to approach; whilst women and boys forced their way about, offering the polluted water of the well for sale, in little glass bottles, the bottom of broken jugs and scallop shells, to those whose strength did not permit them to gain this sacred spot . . .

We left this scene, so calculated to excite compassion and horror, and turned towards the banks of the lake, where whiskey, porter, bread and salmon were sold in booths or tents resembling a gipsy encampment, and formed by means of poles or branches of trees meeting at angles, over which were thrown the proprietor's great coat, his wife's cloak, old blankets, quilts, and occasionally a little straw . . .

Almost every tent had its piper, and two or three young

men and women dancing the jig, or a peculiar kind of dance, called the rinkafadah, which consists of movements by no means graceless or inelegant. The women invariably selected their partners, and went up to the man of their choice, to whom they freely presented their hand. After the dance was concluded, the men dropped a penny each, or, such as were inclined to display their liberality, something more, into an old hat which lay at the piper's feet, or in a hollow made in the ground for the purpose. The piper, who seldom makes a moment's pause, continues playing, and another dance immediately commences . . .

The tents are generally so crowded that the dancers have scarcely room for their performance: from twenty to thirty men and women are often huddled together in each, and the circulation of porter and whiskey amongst the various groups is soon evident in its effects. All become actors, – none spectators, – rebellious songs, in the Irish language, are loudly vociferated, and received with yells of applause: towards evening the tumult increases, and intoxication becomes almost universal. Cudgels are brandished, the shrieks of women and the piercing cry of children thrill painfully upon the ear in the riot and uproar of the scene: indeed the distraction and tumult of a patron cannot be described. At midnight the assembly became somewhat less noisy and confused, but the chapels were still crowded: on the shore, people lay "heads and points" so closely, that it was impossible to move without trampling on them; the washing and bathing in the well still continued, and the dancing, drinking, roaring, and singing were, in some degree, kept up throughout the night. The effect produced by fires lighted early in the evening on the highest points of the surrounding mountains, and reflected in the dark bosom of the lake, was very impressive. Lighting fires, however, on the eve of St. John has not any peculiar reference to the celebration of the patron, being a popular custom of remote antiquity and a remain of Pagan rites in honour of the sun.

THOMAS CROFTON CROKER, *Researches in the South of Ireland*, 1824

St James

26th July Saint James' Day, the Pattern Day of St James' Well, near Callan. Lovely warm day . . . I went with my three youngest children to the pattern. There were gooseberries and currants and cherries for the children; gingerbread for the young girls; strong beer and maddening whiskey for the brawlers and mediators; open-fronted booths full of courting couples; bagpipers and 'scratch-scratch' men playing music for the young people; and devout people doing rounds of the well. The children and I left the well at six o'clock. Crowds of well-dressed people were heading towards it from all directions.

HUMPHREY O'SULLIVAN, *Diary*, 1829
Trans. FRANK MURPHY

St Declan

This hymn in honour of St Declan, patron saint of Ardmore, Co. Waterford, seems to have been written to mark his feast, which falls on 24th June. Its subject and intensity typify the work of Timothy O'Sullivan, whose poems circulated widely in late 18th- and early 19th-century Ireland.

O golden Declan, saintly priest,
    God's people flock to thee;
The clergy sing to mark thy feast,
    And pray on bended knee.

Their solemn way the hillsmen make,
    In grace they pass along;
Heads bowed in prayer, the women take
    Their place within the throng.

St Declan's Well

In distant lands thy holy life
    And teachings bring thee fame;
Give ear, amidst the din and strife
    As we invoke thy name.

For we beneath thy banner fight,
    Which strengthens our belief;
Like soldiers heartened by the sight
    Of their beloved chief.

Our enemies we will bring low
    With God the Father's might;
In triumph from the field we'll go
    Where we defended right.

With huzzahs of delight we'll cry
    To thank the Father's Heir,
Who with His own, our lives did buy
    On Calvary so dear.

On Friday's cross the hammer rang,
  He hung His noble head;
As drop by drop His precious blood
  From ivory palms he shed.

The fires of love, as Heaven's Lord
  His dying seconds ached,
So fierce within her entrails roared,
  That earth herself now quaked.

Were I a saint, or could I preach
  Like Basil, James or Paul,
Augustine, John of golden speech,
  Or had I gifts at all,

To thank the King of Kings my voice
  More worthily I'd raise;
As choirs in Paradise rejoice
  And sing their Master's praise:

But though I've sinned, though I'm not fit
  To rank with learned men,
'Tis what I have of love or wit
  Inspires my simple pen.

O holy mother, who did best
  Our blessed Saviour know,
Who gave Him milk from thine own breast,
  Who saw Him die in woe,

Behold thy children, come to pray
  At Declan's holy place,
And ask thy Son to grant we may
  Soon see him face to face.

TIMOTHY O'SULLIVAN (died 1795)
Trans. FRANK MURPHY

A hurling match

Diversions

Hurling

One exercise they use much is their hurling, which has something in it not unlike the play called Mall. When their cows are casting their hair, they pull it off their backs and with their hands work it into large balls which will grow very hard. This ball they use at the hurlings, which they strike with a stick called commaan about three foot and a half long in the handle. At the lower end it is crooked and about three inches broad, and on this broad part you may sometimes see one of the gamesters carry the ball tossing it for 40 or 50 yards in spite of all the adverse players; and when he is like to lose it, he generally gives it a great stroke to drive it towards the goal. Sometimes if he miss his blow at the ball, he knocks one of the opposers down: at which no resentment is to be shown. They seldom come off without broken heads or shins in which they glory very much. At this sport one parish sometimes or barony challenges another; they pick out ten, twelve or twenty players of a side, and the prize is generally a barrel or two of ale, which is brought into the field and drunk off by the victors on the spot, though the vanquished are not without a share of it too. This commonly is upon some very large plain, the barer of grass the better, and the goals are 200 or 300 yards one from the other; and whichever party drives the ball beyond the other's goal wins the day. Their champions are of the younger and most active among them, and their kindred and mistresses are frequently spectators of their address. Two or three bag pipes attend the conquerors at the barrel's head, and then play them out of the field. At some of these meetings two thousand have been present together.

JOHN DUNTON, *Teague Land, or a Merry Ramble to the Wild Irish,* 1698

Horse Racing

The spot selected for the occasion was the shore of a small bay, which was composed of a fine hard sand, that afforded a very fair and level course for the horses. At the farther end was a lofty pole, on the top of which was suspended by the stirrup a new saddle, the destined guerdon of the conqueror. A red handkerchief, stripped from the neck of Dan Hourigan, the house carpenter, was hoisted overhead, and a crowd of country people dressed, notwithstanding the fineness of the day, in their heavy frieze great coats, stood round the winning-post, each faction being resolved to see justice done to its own representative in the match. A number of tents, composed of old sheets, bags and blankets, with a pole at the entrance, and a sheaf of reed, a broken bottle, or a sod of turf, erected for a sign, were discernible among the multitude that thronged the side of the little rising ground before mentioned. High above the rest Mick Normal's sign-board waved in the rising wind. Busy was the look of that lean old man, as he bustled to and fro among his pigs, kegs, mugs, pots and porringers. A motley mass of felt hats, white muslin caps and ribbons, scarlet cloaks, and blue riding-jocks, filled up the spaces between the tents, and moved in a continual series of involutions, whirls, and eddies, like those which are observable on the surface of a fountain newly filled. The horses were to start from the end of the bay, opposite to the winning-post, go round Mick Normal's tent, and the cowel on the hill side, and returning to the place from whence they came, run straight along the sand for the saddle. This was to be the victor's prize.

GERALD GRIFFIN, *The Collegians,* 1829

Sea Bathing

A traveller takes the road from Sligo to Boyle.

I was surprised to meet, every few hundred yards on this road, carts heavily laden with country people, many of them of the lowest orders, and, with different articles of furniture piled upon, or attached to the carts; and I learned, with some astonishment, that all these individuals were on their way to sea-bathing. This is a universal practice over these parts of Ireland. A few weeks passed at the sea-side is looked upon to be absolutely necessary for the preservation of health; and persons, of all classes, migrate thither, with their families. In my way to Boyle, I met upwards of twenty carts laden with women, children, and boys. One may ask how the people afford this annual expense? but the expense is extremely small. There are numerous cabins and cottages, at the lower end of Sligo, on the bay, in which a room is hired at 1s. 6d. per week. This is almost the whole of the expense; for all carry with them, besides their beds and an iron pot, – a quantity of meal, some sacks of potatos, and even turf, if there be room for it.

HENRY D. INGLIS, *Journey Throughout Ireland,* 1834

Sweating Houses

The 'sweating-house' here described was in Ulster.

I had heard of a peculiar practice of the inhabitants of this part of the country, and I desired to make some inquiries about it. I refer to what are called 'Sweating-Houses,' which are looked upon here as a remedy for all ills. Mr. Hamilton was good enough to take me to see one in the neighbourhood. I am sure it will trouble the reader to imagine what a sweating-house can be, and for his benefit I may say it is a species of oven five or six feet high by about three in width, with a hole for entrance of about one and a half feet high at the level of the earth, the whole construction being the shape of a thimble.

To use the sweating-house they heat it with turf, exactly in the way such a construction would be heated for the purpose of baking bread. When it is pretty hot, four or five men or women, entirely naked, creep in as best they can through the little opening, which is immediately closed with a piece of wood covered over with dung. The unfortunates stay in this for four or five hours without the possibility of getting out, and if one of them takes ill, he or she may sit down, but the plank will not be taken away before the proper time. As soon as the patients enter, an abundant perspiration starts, and, commonly, when they come out they are much thinner than when they went in. Wherever there are four of five cabins near each other there is sure to be a sweating-house, and no matter what may be the malady of the peasant, he uses this as a means of cure. The man who showed me the one I examined had been in it the day before for sore eyes.

To know exactly what it felt like to be in one I crept in myself, and although no fire had been in it for twenty-four hours, and although the hole through which I crept remained open, I must say that there are few maladies which I would not prefer to the sweating-house remedy.

DE LA TOCNAYE, *Promenade d'un Français dans l'Irlande*, 1797

Dancing

Among the Poor

DANCING is very general among the poor people, almost universal in every cabbin. Dancing-masters of their own rank travel through the country from cabbin to cabbin, with a piper or blind fiddler; and the pay is six pence a quarter. It is an absolute system of education. Weddings are always celebrated with much dancing; and a Sunday rarely passes without a dance; there are very few among them who will not, after a hard day's work, gladly walk seven miles to have a dance. *John* is not so lively; but then a hard day's work with him is certainly a different affair from what it is with *Paddy*.

ARTHUR YOUNG, A Tour in Ireland, 1776–79

'*Dancing in Ireland, like everything else connected with the amusement of the people, is frequently productive of bloodshed.*'
William Carleton (1830–33)

A Rustic Group

We met a truly rustic group; the young men and women of the village were enjoying themselves by a dance; a fiddler and a piper emulously lent their strains, which were not ill bestowed upon their hearers, for they shewed, by their rude jokes and merry glee, how open the mind is to music, even of the coarsest kind. Each young man as he took his partner gave an halfpenny to the piper, and then set too with all their heart and soul.

G. HOLMES, *Sketches of Some of the Southern Counties of Ireland,* 1797

On Red Turf Hill

12th July A thousand young women and young men were danc-ing to music on Red Turf Hill.

HUMPHREY O'SULLIVAN, *Diary,* 1827
Trans. FRANK MURPHY

Soirées dansantes

The writer of these lines was a guest of Daniel O'Connell at Derry-nane; the love of dancing was evidently not restricted to the peasantry.

The drawing-room was very large, and served as a ballroom every night, for there was a numerous party of dancing people now in the house. How gay were those pleasant *soirées dansantes!* No matter what had been the fatigues of the morning, dancing was supposed the best remedy for them.

CATHERINE M. O'CONNELL, *Excursions in Ireland,* 1844

Never a Dull Moment

25th November I have not been out for a fortnight, except for the evenings when I went for walks to the fair-green, and down to the Avonbeg, like the owl, bird of the night and the air. And the reason for my staying indoors by day is that I have one black eye and another even blacker, which I got from Dr. Butler on the evening of Sunday the eleventh day of this month, or perhaps it was early on the Monday morning.

This is how it happened. I was with a group of friends drinking at Margaret Commerton's. We had plenty of warm whiskey and sugar to drink. Thomas O'Kelly, a young trader, began to wrestle with John Forastal, a medical student. Thomas O'Looney, another medical student, thinking it was a fight, hit O'Kelly in the face and knocked him to the floor. Up got O'Kelly, and not knowing who had hit him, began trouncing everyone in his path and struck John Hearn, a young gentleman, who gave him a beating in return, blackening his small keen eye.

Then all of a sudden we were joined by Michael O'Manton, a scratch-scratch man or fiddler, in his shirtsleeves, so that we were fighting like boars . . . Finally, Margaret and I succeeded in making peace among the sturdy warriors.

'Poor thing, dearie, you've got two black eyes,' said gentle Margaret to Thomas O'Kelly.

'In that case I'm like you,' said O'Kelly, 'for even ripe sloes are not as black as your black eyes, with their beautiful black lashes and eyebrows; and the blackbird, when he sings in May, is not as sweet as your sweet red-lipped mouth; and now for a nice little kiss, my sweetheart, while I'm near you.' And with that, he gave her a loud kiss which resounded like a wet shoe dropped on a hot stove.

So we took our leave of O'Kelly, and left him courting gentle Margaret. Off we went to Sinclair's tavern; he's the old soldier who hails from Scotland, but he's English, not a Scottish Gael. O'Manton began playing his 'scratch-scratch'. John Hearn and a few others began dancing wildly. Oldis joined in, looking like a swallow on a branch, with his crooked legs. We were having a grand time of it when Butler rushed in like a madman, a black-thorn stick in one hand, his other hand adjusting the angle of his hat, the devil of a grimace on his face and his eyes burning with the flames of war.

'When the cat's away, the mice will play,' said Butler. At this O'Looney and Forastal ran outside, Hearn ran into the ash-heap, someone else ran into the coal-heap, which left Oldis dancing, O'Manton playing his scratch-scratch, and myself, a fool if ever there was one, sitting on my bench.

'Away with your scratch-scratch! You'll wake up the geese. Stick your tool in your bag and put your bag on your back,' said Butler.

'No I won't,' said Oldis.

'I'll make you do it,' said Butler, 'and you'll pay for this [?], you damned drunkard.'

'Easier said than done!' said Oldis, 'we can all see who's drunk!'

With that, mad Butler made a grab for Oldis's beard and hair, pulling him to the ground. Not to be outdone, Oldis seized Butler's legs and dragged him down in the dirty ale and whiskey which were spilt all over the floor, where they began tearing and tugging and tussling each other like mad dogs till they were separated. No sooner was mad Butler on his feet than he raced towards O'Manton who was huddling in the ash-heap, threw him down on the dirty floor, and they began punching and pounding and pummelling each other with their fists, in the side, in the lips, in the eyes, kicking each other in the shins, till they were both bruised and bashed and battered, a mass of skin and flesh and bones when they were separated. Then Butler looked at me sitting on the stool, and swooping down on me like a wolf on a hawk or a lark, before I could offer any defence, he struck me with his fist, giving me a black eye – in the twinkling of an eye, so to speak. I fell to the ground, like a slaughtered ox. Not content with this, mad Butler attacked again, and blackened the other eye.

'Punch him up, every inch of him,' said the lady of the house, the lady innkeeper, a big-bellied brazen blubbery bitch, with bulging buttocks, flat flabby feet, paps as obscene as the tits of an old cow, great rough lips, flat snub-nose, teeth like tobacco-cloves, red watery eyes with bags beneath them and heavy wet lashes above. 'Punch every bit of him, soft and hard, till his mother won't know any part of him,' said this devil in woman's shape.

But with the help of my friends I escaped from mad Butler, and came home in a sorry state. And by my bum, as Giolla an Amarain would say, I won't be going back to a tavern for a very long time.

That is how I got the black eyes which have kept me prisoner here for the past fortnight, without seeing a leaf, fresh or withered, without hearing the murmuring stream or the roaring waves, or the bellowing ox, or the winter wind whistling through the trees.

HUMPHREY O'SULLIVAN, *Diary,* 1827
Trans. FRANK MURPHY

BY THE FIRESIDE

Pancake tossing

Early 19th-century Ireland must have been like modern Belgium, in one respect at least. Two languages, *Béarla* and *Gaeilge*, existed side by side in the same country and often in the same landscape, as do Flemish Dutch and Walloon French. After six hundred years of colonial rule, English was so entrenched that the Irish word *béarla*, which originally meant 'speech' or 'language', had come to mean 'English', as distinct from all other languages. English was, so to speak, language with a capital L.

But *Gaeilge* had by no means disappeared. In about 1815 a traveller's directory warned that:

In Ireland, four fifths of the population of Connaught, Munster, and the north-west of Ulster still speak Irish . . . ; in the other counties of Ulster and Leinster it is used as the family language, by more than one half . . . Tourists should not be surprized if the swains of Ireland should commit some blunders in speaking English. *

---

* A. M. Graham, *The Post Chaise Companion, or Traveller's Directory Through Ireland*, Dublin, c. 1815, p. ix.

A traveller noted in 1837, 'I addressed many people who did not understand a word of English',* while on the eve of the Famine, Catherine O'Connell wrote in describing a quay in Cork:

We see . . . a very old woman, and around her are men and women in the vigour of youth, and sturdy children, all busy among piles of luggage, for they are all about to emigrate.
On addressing the old woman she tells us, 'I've no English'; and except these words she can say nothing in that language. The tears course down her cheeks as in her native tongue she laments the home she is leaving, and having to lay her bones in a strange country . . .†

When these words were written in the 1840s, there were more speakers of Irish than at any previous time in history. But unlike Belgium, where French and Dutch compete on roughly equal terms, at this period in Ireland the long struggle between Irish and English was almost over. Evicted from the public domain, from government and commerce, from school and church, Irish retreated to the private domain, to the peasant's cabin. In the significant words of the traveller's directory quoted above, it was 'the family language', but nothing more.

In the dank climate of the Emerald Isle, the focus of family and social life was the hearth (*focus*, in Latin). It is with good reason that Irish has a saying *Nil aon tinteán mar do thinteán féin*, which means literally 'There's no hearth like your own hearth'.

'Focal' point of the house, the turf-fire burned not only all year, but often from year to year without going out. In its flickering shadows the Irish language reigned supreme: strangers were made welcome according to the rules of Irish hospitality; neighbours delivered the latest gossip; family disputes flared up and died away; children learned to sing the old songs, or listened spell-bound as grand-uncle Seamus told the stories he had heard

---

* Leitch Ritchie, *Ireland Picturesque and Romantic,* Longman, Rees, Orme, Brown, Green and Longman, London, 1837, p. 131.
† Catherine M. O'Connell, *Excursions in Ireland during 1844 and 1850,* A. Bentley, London, 1852, p. 242.

as a child in the same house eighty years before. Poor as they were in other ways, the common people were rich in words, which cost nothing. They delighted to repeat a proverb or a deft rejoinder, and knew countless songs by heart; they revered the story-teller. Like the Australian Aborigines, they palliated their hardships by creating a world of the imagination through the almost boundless resources of language.

Candlestick from Northern Ireland, for burning the peeled rush soaked in tallow

Hospitality

Irish Brogues

Among the old Irish, a stranger had no more to do in order to introduce himself, than to sit by the fire and put off his brogues, which custom is preserved to this day in the more uncivilized parts of this country; such a person was entitled to the laws of hospitality, and reckoned one of the family; and if a second stranger came in, he took upon himself to bid him welcome, with as much freedom as if he was master of the house.

CHARLES SMITH, *The Antient and Present State of the City and County of Cork*, 1750

Cabin Hospitality

The habits of cabin life and cabin hospitality have so much sameness, that the specimen which follows may answer for the whole. About seven one evening I reached the cabin of a woman whose daughter had been a servant in my house in New York. In a corner, where a bed might have stood, was a huge bank of turf, and a pile of straw for the pigs. There was but one room beside, and the family consisted of some five or six individuals. The cabin door being open the pigs, geese, ducks, hens, and dogs walked in and out at option.

After the usual warm greeting, the girl was bidden to go out and dig some potatoes; the pot was hung over the fire, the potatoes boiled, the table was removed into the adjoining room, and a touch from the finger of the matron was the signal for me to follow her into supper. On a naked deal table stood a plate of potatoes and a mug of milk. The potatoes must be eaten from the hand, without knife, fork, or plate; and the milk taken in sups from the mug. I applied my nails to divesting the potato of its coat, and my hostess urged the frequent use of the milk, saying, 'It was provided on purpose for you, and you must take it.' It must be remembered that a sup of sweet milk among the poor in Ireland, is as much a rarity and a luxury as a slice of plum-pudding in a farmhouse in America. After supper we returned to the kitchen.

The good man of the house soon entered, and gave me as hearty a welcome as an Irishman could give; and the neighbouring women and children gathered in, till the pile of turf and every stool was occupied. A cheerful peat fire was burning upon the hearth; the children were snugly cowered in each corner; two large pigs walked in, and adjusted their nest upon the straw; two or three straggling hens were about the room, which the woman caught, and raising the broken lid of a chest in one end of the apartment, she put them in; the dog was bidden to drive out the

Girl from Co. Leitrim

geese; the door was shut, and the man then turning to me, said, 'You see how these pigs know their place, and when it's a little cowld not a ha'p'orth of 'em will stay out of doors; and we always keep a handful of straw in that corner for their bed.' The company seemed quite inclined to stay; but the good woman, looking well to my comfort, called me at an early hour to the next room, and pointing to a bed which had been erected for my accommodation, said, 'This troop here would be talking all night; ye must be tired, and see what I've got for ye.' This was a bed fixed upon chairs, and made so wide that two could occupy it; and she assured me that so glad was she to see me, that she would sleep in a part of it by my side. It was certainly an extra extension of civility to leave the good man, who, by the way, had two daughters and a son of sixteen to sleep under the same covering, and in the same room with us. His bed was made of a bundle or two of straw spread upon rough sticks, and a decent woollen covering put over it.

A. NICHOLSON, *The Bible in Ireland*, 1844–45

Definitions

Culled from Dinneen's Dictionary, these words give an idea of the raw materials which the story-teller – or for that matter any speaker of Irish – had at his disposal.

bothantaidheacht (fem.): the practice of frequenting the neighbours' houses for the purpose of hearing old stories, etc. (Kerry).

búr (masc.): a boor, a term for the English.

cailleach (fem.): an old woman, a hag; a fisherman's stone anchor; a fir stump found in bogs; a bad or shrivelled potato.

dán (masc.): a rope tied around a cow's horns to prevent her going overboard (in shipping) (Aran).

drúichtín (masc.): a light dew; a species of small whitish snail. On May morning girls discovered the colour of the hair of their future husbands from the shade of colouring of the first *drúichtín* they found.

feadghoile (fem.): a noise made in the stomach of some horses when trotting.

fionnán (masc.): a kind of long coarse white grass which grows on marshy land, used for making grass ropes (*súgán*) and as bedding for cattle.

gad (masc.): a withe; a twisted twig or osier; *cladhaire gaid*, a villain fit for the gallows. It would seem as if victims were formerly hanged by means of withes.

gaedhealach (adj.): Irish, Gaelic; *also* Irish-made, simple, unsophisti-cated, easy-going; common, native.

glasghaibhlinn: very green grass, through which water generally runs (Derry); the grass which produces the best milk; *cf. an Ghlas-Ghaibhlinn*, a celebrated cow which could never be fully milked . . .

maighre (masc.): a salmon; *fig.* a fine healthy person; *often* a proud woman; *maighre cailín*, a fine, handsome girl; *maighre buachalla*, a handsome, strong lad.

reilig (fem.): a church, a churchyard, a grave; *réabadh reilge*, an uproot-ing and consequent desecration of a burial-ground, which was con-sidered a crime to be visited with sudden punishment; *cam reilge*, the defect of being bandy-legged, from a superstition that a pregnant woman treading on a grave gives birth to a bandy-legged child.

sniugadh (masc.): the last and richest part of an animal's milk; the act of milking the very last drop.

spadán (masc.): lea-land on which potatoes are grown by spread-ing them on the unprepared surface and covering them over with soil taken from the furrows.

stócach (masc.): a stake, a pole; a ship's mast; *fig.* a tall young fellow; an idler; one who lives on others; the person that accom-panies a man looking for a wife at Shrovetide (Kerry).

REV. PATRICK DINNEEN, *Irish-English Dictionary*, 1904

Greetings

The custom of greeting with a benediction has been practised in Ireland from time immemorial . . .

Persons on a journey are saluted with various and peculiar phrases, appropriate to the time of day, the nature of the road they are pursuing, or other circumstances. Early in the morning, or on the approach of night, you hear such as 'God speed you', 'God and the Blessed Virgin attend you', 'The blessed Patrick go with you', &c.; but if the traveller has to apprehend danger on his route, the expressions are more energetic, as 'Safe home to you by the help of God', 'God guide and protect you, and lead you in safety to your own home, with the blessing of all the Saints.'

THOMAS CROFTON CROKER, *Researches in the South of Ireland*, 1824

Proverbs and Sayings

The Leinsterman affable,
The Munsterman boastful,
The Connachtman sweet-mouthed,
And the Ulsterman proud.

The way of the nuns with the country-women – they receive a great lump and give a small return.

The seat of a son in his father's house is a broad comfortable seat, but the seat of the father in his son's house is a round unstable seat.

If you wish to be reviled, marry;
If you wish to be praised, die.

The coldness of a friend is better than the sweetness of any enemy.

She has not burned seven turf stacks with him yet. (Said of a couple not long married.)

It is better to be lucky than wise.

He who takes longest to eat will live the longest.

Any condiment at all is better than to be eating potatoes dry.

Butter with butter is no condiment.

There are slippery stones at the doors of the rich.

You'll be a good messenger to send for death. (To one taking his time on an errand.)

When your neighbour's house is on fire, take care of your own.

Don't break your shin on a stool that is not in your way.

May the face of every good news, and the back of every bad news be towards us.

It is a wedge from itself that splits the oak. (That is, a small group of seceders from a group or family can do more harm than all the forces of the enemy.)

The friendship of the Callans – the heat of the oaten bread. (Which comes very hot from the fire, but cools very quickly.)

One Finegan is enough for the side of a parish. (They were supposed to be quarrelsome.)

I saw O'Toole's castle and O'Toole himself. (Said by someone who has just escaped some dread calamity.)

May we have the grace of God, and die in Ireland.

Traditional
Trans. ENRI UA MUIRGHEASA

Wit

The native wit and humour of the low Irish is singularly happy. A beggar had been for a long time besieging an old, gouty, testy, limping gentleman, who refused his mite with great irritability, upon which the mendicant said, 'Ah, plaze your honour's honour, I wish God had made your *heart* as tender as your *toes*' . . .

It is always a source of pleasure to listen to the conversation of the lower Irish; at these places, wit, drollery, or strength of expression, is sure to be reward of it. 'I am very bad, Pat,' said one poor fellow, rubbing his head, to another. 'Ah! then may God keep you so, for fear of being worse,' was the reply . . .

Many years ago, a gentleman of consequence and interest was tried at the assizes of Galway for murder, and, notwith-

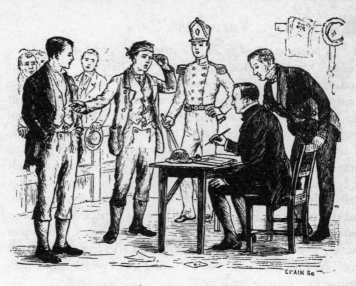

Plaintiff and defendant before a magistrate in Co. Galway

standing the clearest evidence of the facts, the jury acquitted him. Soon afterwards, as some gentlemen were standing at a large window at Lucas's Coffee-house, much resorted to in those days, a criminal was carried past to be executed; upon which they said, 'What is that fellow going to be hanged for?' A low fellow who was passing by, and overheard the question, looked up and said, 'Plaze your honours! for want of a Galway jury!'

JOHN CARR, *The Stranger in Ireland*, 1805

Curses

Two Maledictions

A grievous imprecation in the Irish language is 'May your burial be forsaken': they also have another very figurative malediction 'May the grass grow green before your door'.

JOHN CARR, *The Stranger in Ireland*, 1805

The Smith's Curse

In . . . a poem ascribed to Saint Patrick, we find Patrick calling on 'the Might of God, the power of God, the wisdom of God, the eye of God, the ear of God, the word of God, the hand of God, the shield of God,' etc., to protect him against the 'spells of women and of SMITHS and of Druids.' When people, who had only bronze or brass before, first got to know of iron, they naturally enough marvelled at it, and believed there was an invisible virtue in it. Probably they afterwards got to believe that some of this wonderful power and virtue that was in the iron was also in the smith who worked the iron, and this belief has lasted from the time of Patrick down to our own day. Accordingly if a person desires to put a curse upon another person he goes to the smith and asks him 'to turn the anvil' on his enemy, so that a melting and every kind of misfortune may come upon him.

DOUGLAS HYDE, *Religious Songs of Connacht*, 1906

Days of the Brindled Cow

The modern or Gregorian calendar came into effect in 1582 A.D. By the 19th century, there was a difference of twelve days between the Old Style and the New.

12th April Today is the twelfth day of April, the first of the three days of the old brindled cow i.e. three days which Old March took from the beginning of Old April. The story runs as follows:
There was an old brindled cow in the olden days which had got through the month of March without falling into a bog-hole or swamp, and when the first day of Old April came, she put her tail up in the air and ran about bellowing with joy because the warm weather had come and she was safe and sound, after raw harsh windy March, 'Wait! Wait!' said Old March, and the blusterer came to visit mild April, and asked her for three days.

'I will give them to you,' said April, 'if you will marry me.'

'I will,' said rough March to gentle April. And the hard harsh fierce piercing wind blew down from the heights of Scotland, and the old brindled cow went off looking for soft green grass growing by the swamp, and she drowned. Hence the expression 'the days of the brindled cow'...

HUMPHREY O'SULLIVAN, *Diary*, 1827
Trans. FRANK MURPHY

Folktales

The three stories given here are as written down by scholars in the early part of this century, but come from a very old oral tradition.

The Prince and the Well

A story from Lough Leane, largest of the three lakes of Killarney.

There was once a prince of the O'Donoghues called Domhnall, a stout-hearted and generous fellow who ruled his people wisely from his great city at the foot of the mountains. Near this city was the prince's palace, which lay in the middle of a rich plain. In this plain there grew luxuriant trees which reached into the sky. There was also in this plain a well of very fresh, very sweet spring-water, whose like was to be found nowhere in Ireland. But there was magic on it, and it was said all through the land that if the well were to be left without its lid even for one night, it would spread all over the place, drowning the city and all its people. Hence from olden times, it had always been covered with a great stone lid at night.

But one night after he had drunk much wine, Domhnall frightened the company by saying that he believed none of what was said about the well, and that he would make them all understand that it was an old wives' tale from start to finish. He sent for the stone lid to the well, and kept it in his court that evening. It was no use opposing the prince: his wishes had to be carried out. So all the people trembled in fear as they waited for the well-water to break out, except one man whose terror was so great that he fled to the hills. During the night the water broke out, and when the survivor looked back in the morning, he saw neither house nor city nor plain; there was nothing but a great lake which covered everything, lapping against the mountain-sides, or roaring wildly whenever there was a storm.

But the people had not perished, not a single one of them. For their splendid city still lies beneath the water, and now and again fishermen catch a glimpse of them as they stare into the water in the stillness of evening. Now and again, till this very day – once in every seven years, the local people say – Domhnall himself comes onto the land, and his coming is an omen of happiness and prosperity for that year . . . and his visit is often followed by terrible storms. The manner in which he comes is not always the same. Sometimes – say those who have seen him – he comes riding on a white mare across the lake, splendidly attired and with a company of retainers. At other times he is seated in a boat borne on the waves. Sometimes he comes on to the land and plays hurling with the lads; at other times he nimbly takes part in the long dance. He is dressed in red, and wears a three-cornered hat. There is not a stone nor a headland nor an island nor a rock throughout the lake which does not have some link with Domhnall O'Donoghue. His library is here, his bed there, his table somewhere else.

Traditional, from REV. PATRICK DINNEEN, *Killarney,* 1902
Trans. FRANK MURPHY

The Two Hunchbacks

Once upon a time there were two men in Galway, whose names were John O'Neill and Paddy O'Kelly, and both had been hunchbacked since they were boys.

John was coming home one day, and it happened that as he was passing by a rath, he heard a voice inside the rath saying:

'Monday and Tuesday!
Monday and Tuesday!'
John stood listening.
'Monday and Tuesday and Wednesday!
Monday and Tuesday and Wednesday!' said John.
'Who is singing my song?' said the man inside.
'I am,' said John.
'Come inside then,' he said, 'and whatever you ask for, you may have.'

A door opened for John, and he went inside. He was asked what he would like.

'Well,' he said, 'I would like my hump to be taken from me.'
'I will be happy to do that for you,' said the man in the rath.

He fell on him, and before John knew what was happening, he had taken his hump from him. He seized the hump and hung it on the wall.

'Make your way home now,' he said to John. 'All's well now.'

John went home, overjoyed at having his hump removed. When the people of the village saw him coming, they were startled because he was as straight as a gun-barrel, without a hump, without stooping, and it was not long before Paddy O'Kelly heard about it. He came to John and asked him how he had lost his hump.

'Well,' said John, 'I was walking past the rath over there, and I heard a voice saying:
"Monday and Tuesday!
Monday and Tuesday!"
"Monday and Tuesday and Wednesday!
Monday and Tuesday and Wednesday!" I said.
"Who is singing my song?" said the voice.
"John O'Neill," I said. Then he called me in, and told me I could have whatever I wanted. So I asked him to take my hump from me, and he made me as you see me now.'

'Good Lord!' said Paddy, 'I'll go to the rath tomorrow and have my hump taken from me.'

So the next morning off Paddy went to the rath, and when he reached it, he heard the voice saying:

'Monday, Tuesday, Wednesday,
Every day is weaving day;
Monday, Tuesday, Wednesday,
Every day is weaving day!'

'Monday, Tuesday, Wednesday, Thursday, Friday, Saturday, and Sunday!

Monday, Tuesday, Wednesday, Thursday, Friday, Saturday, and Sunday!' said Paddy O'Kelly.

'Who's spoiling my song?' said the man inside.

'I am,' said Paddy O'Kelly.

'Come inside and I'll do something for you,' he said.

Paddy went inside, and when the man in the rath saw him, what did he do but seize the hump he had taken from John O'Neill and put it on top of the other hump. So out he came from the rath and set off home, sad and sorrowful with his two humps.

If the people of the village had been startled to see John O'Neil coming home without his hump, they were seven times more startled when they saw Paddy coming with two.

Chance favoured John but not Paddy, and it would have been better for Paddy to stay at home and suffer his one hump, than to have two humps on his back till the day he died.

Traditional
Trans. FRANK MURPHY

The Connaughtman Who went to Ulster

After the rebellion of Cahir O'Doherty, many Englishmen came to Ulster and settled as farmers on the land. At that time a young man from Connaught went there looking for work. He saw a young farmboy coming out of a farmhouse, with blood streaming down both his cheeks. When the Connaughtman asked him what had happened, the young man replied, 'The farmer here is exploiting his farmboys: he has baskets full of ears that he has cut off farmboys whom he deceives with a bargain that he makes with them. He promises them that, if they should see him angry before the cuckoo calls, he will give them ten pounds and let them cut off both his ears. But if they become angry, he will cut off their ears, and send them on their way without a penny. He gives only one meal a day, and this is his way of winning.'

'We'll see about that,' said the Connaughtman. He went inside; the bargain was soon made. He was given his dinner, and as he knew from the man who had lost his ears that there would be nothing else to eat, he put the leftovers in his pockets.

He went out to the barn to thresh barley. The farmer had no-one with him but his mother and himself; she was old and grey. When night fell, the Connaughtman stopped work and came inside; not a word was said to him about supper; he went off to sleep in the corner, and ate the food in his pockets.

When he began to eat, the old crone said to her son, 'I'll warrant he's a Connaughtman.'

When he rose next morning, he was told to return to the barn, and he winnowed barley there till he had filled two sacks. Seeing a carter going along the road, he called him over and said, 'Take these two sacks and sell them, and fetch me the best quarter of beef you can find, and two bottles of whiskey, and be back by dinner-time.'

As soon as he had the whiskey and the beef, he made a fire and began to roast the beef. When the farmer smelt the meat cooking, he came and said, 'Connaughtman! Where did you get all this meat and whiskey?'

The Connaughtman said, 'I sold two sacks of barley to the carter, who gave me these things in return. Are you angry?'

'Oh no! I'm not angry,' said the farmer. 'Are you angry, Connaughtman?'

'No, why should I be?' said the young man, tearing off a piece of meat and eating it. 'This is the best job I've ever had.'

The farmer went back inside and told the old crone about the meat and whiskey which the Connaughtman had.

'Ah,' said the crone,' 'you won't have a farthing left, unless I fix him tomorrow. Tell him to take out the two horses in the stable which have never been harnessed and plough with them tomorrow. That will make him angry, and then you'll be able to cut off his ears and send him on his way.'

In the morning the Connaughtman took the two horses and harnesssed them together with the plough behind. They began squealing and lashing. He saw a tin-merchant coming along the road with two old white nags, and said to him, 'I'll exchange these two horses for your two white ones.'

He was happy with this. The young man harnessed the two white nags and began ploughing. They were so worn out that their bones came through their skin.

The farmer came and said, 'Connaughtman! Where are my two horses that you took out this morning?'

The Connaughtman said, 'Here they are, and all yours. I couldn't get any use out of the other two, and made an exchange with the tin-merchant, and here they are working nicely.'

'You've ruined me,' said the farmer.

'Are you angry?' asked the Connaughtman, eating his meat.

'Oh no!' said the farmer, 'I'm not angry. Are you angry, Connaughtman?'

'On no!' said he, 'Why should I be?' as he drank from his bottle.

The farmer told the old crone how the horses were gone, and she said, 'I'll fix him tomorrow. Tell him to cover the road in front of the house with the costliest cloths he can find, as your relatives are coming from England to visit you, and to be finished by evening, and that is sure to make him angry.'

As soon as the sun was up so was the Connaughtman. He breakfasted on roast meat and whiskey. Then he took a great long-handled hatchet, and gathered the bullocks and heifers from the farm into a secure place. He struck one of them with the hatchet, killed it, skinned it and spread the skin on the road. Then he killed the animals one by one until there was a covering of skins on the roadway. When the farmer came in the evening, he saw the slaughter the Connaughtman had done, and said, 'What sort of job is this?'

'A good job, master,' said the Connaughtman. 'The costliest cloths I could find to put on the road were the skins of your bullocks and heifers.'

'You've ruined me,' said the farmer.

'Are you angry?' asked the Connaughtman.

'Oh no!' said the farmer. "Are you angry, Connaughtman?' he asked.

'I'm not angry,' answered the Connaughtman, 'Why should I be?' And he took the bottle from his pocket to drink from it.

The old crone said, 'I'll use enchantment tomorrow, and make myself into a cuckoo. I'll go up into the holly-bush in front of the window and start singing so that you'll both hear me. Then you'll be able to pay him and send him away.'

As soon as the sun was up so was the old crone. She made herself into a cuckoo and went into the holly-bush, and said, 'Cuckoo, cuckoo!' until the Connaughtman heard her. He seized the gun, fired it, and down she fell from the bush.

The farmer came to him and said, 'Connaughtman! What have you done now?'

'A good deed,' answered the Connaughtman. 'That can't have been a real cuckoo, singing between All Saints' Day and Christmas. Cuckoos have never been known to sing then.'

'But you've just killed my mother!' said the farmer.

'You're angry,' answered the Connaughtman.

'I am,' said the farmer, 'and with good reason: you've killed my mother.'

'I'll cut off both your ears, and a piece of your cheek.'

'Don't, Connaughtman! and I'll give you a thousand pounds, and your wages in full.'

The farmer gave him the money, and he went off home and married a fine girl who owned plenty of land. Their children can still be found in County Mayo, where they live rich and contented.

Traditional
Trans. FRANK MURPHY

The Aisling

In 18th- and early 19th-century Ireland, one of the best-loved poetic forms was the *aisling* or vision-poem. In this the poet wanders, forlorn, brooding on his misfortunes and those of his people. Suddenly he beholds a young woman whose beauty is almost unbearable, and realises that she is the spirit of Ireland. As he listens she laments her fate, then foretells the downfall of the English, the return of Ireland's true (Stuart) King, the restoration of the old Gaelic order.

One of the greatest writers of *aislingi* was Egan O'Rahilly, a contemporary of J. S. Bach, and like him a master of conventions that pall quickly in less skilful hands. He is proud to speak with the traditional public voice of the Irish poet, but does so in a sad, personal tone. In one of his poems, for example, Ireland is like a woman 'without a husband, without a son, without a spouse'; she is stripped naked, the dogs of Bristol drink her heart's blood, her trees have been burnt and broken down, Blarney is inhabited by wolves, and in the Binding or Envoi, he tells us how:

Every family of those that loved my class, how they are scorned:
This has brought me still poor, lacking shoes, to town today.

O'Rahilly makes up for his poverty in the opulence and inventiveness of his language, which is not easy to translate.

This version of one of his best poems falls a long way short of the original, but is difficult to surpass. The 'clown' is presumably the English king.

The Brightest of the Bright met me on my path so lonely;
    The Crystal of all Crystals was her flashing dark-blue eye;
Melodious more than music was her spoken language only;
    And glorious were her cheeks, of a brilliant crimson dye.

With ringlets above ringlets her hair in many a cluster
    Descended to the earth, and swept the dewy flowers;
Her bosom shone as bright as a mirror in its lustre;
    She seemed like some fair daughter of the Celestial Powers.

She chanted me a chant, a beautiful and grand hymn,
    Of him who should be shortly Eire's reigning King –
She prophesied the fall of the wretches who had banned him;
    And somewhat else she told me which I dare not sing.

Trembling with many fears I called on Holy Mary,
    As I drew nigh this Fair, to shield me from all harm,
When, wonderful to tell! she fled far to the Fairy
    Green mansions of Sliabh Luachra in terror and alarm.

O'er mountain, moor and marsh, by green wood, lough and hollow,
    I tracked her distant footsteps with a throbbing heart;
Through many an hour and day did I follow on and follow,
    Till I reached the magic palace reared of old by Druid art.

There a wild and wizard band with mocking fiendish laughter
    Pointed out me her I sought, who sat low beside a clown;
And I felt as though I never could dream of Pleasure after
    When I saw the maid so fallen whose charms deserved a crown.

Then with burning speech and soul, I looked at her and told her
    That to wed a churl like that was for her the shame of shames
When a bridegroom such as I was longing to enfold her
    To a bosom that her beauty had enkindled into flames.

But answer made she none; she wept with bitter weeping,
   Her tears ran down in rivers, but nothing could she say;
She gave me then a guide for my safe and better keeping, –
   The Brightest of the Bright, whom I met upon my way.

EGAN O'RAHILLY (c.1675-1729)
Trans. JAMES CLARENCE MANGAN

Dark Rosaleen

Tout se termine par une chanson: everything ends with a song, say the French. And a book on the Irish, whose love of song is well known, could do worse than to exemplify this saying. Here to conclude is Mangan's version of the popular *Róisín Dubh* in which, as in an *aisling*, the woman whom the singer addresses (Dark Rosaleen, or Little Black Rose), is generally thought to represent Ireland.

O my dark Rosaleen,
   Do not sigh, do not weep!
The priests are on the ocean green,
   They march along the deep.
There's wine from the royal Pope,
   Upon the ocean green;
And Spanish ale shall give you hope,
   My dark Rosaleen!
   My own Rosaleen!
Shall glad your heart, shall give you hope,
Shall give you health and help, and hope,
   My dark Rosaleen.

Over hills, and through dales,
   Have I roamed for your sake;
All yesterday I sailed with sails
   On river and on lake.
The Erne, at its highest flood,
   I dashed across unseen,
For there was lightning in my blood,

My dark Rosaleen!
My own Rosaleen!
Oh! there was lightning in my blood,
Red lightning lightened through my blood,
   My dark Rosaleen!

All day long in unrest,
   To and fro do I move,
   The very soul within my breast
   Is wasted for you, love!
The heart in my bosom faints
   To think of you, my Queen,
My life of life, my saint of saints,
   My dark Rosaleen!
   My own Rosaleen!
To hear, your sweet and sad complaints,
My life, my love, my saint of saints,
   My dark Rosaleen!

Woe and pain, pain and woe,
   Are my lot, night and noon,
To see your bright face clouded so,
   Like to the mournful moon.
But yet will I rear your throne
   Again in golden sheen;
'Tis you shall reign, shall reign alone,
   My dark Rosaleen!
   My own Rosaleen!
'Tis you shall have the golden throne,
'Tis you shall reign, shall reign alone,
   My dark Rosaleen!

Over dews, over sands,
   Will I fly for your weal:
Your holy, delicate white hands
   Shall girdle me with steel.

At home in your emerald bowers,
  From morning's dawn till e'en,
You'll pray for me, my flower of flowers,
  My dark Rosaleen!
  My fond Rosaleen!
You'll think of me through daylight's hours,
My virgin flower, my flower of flowers,
  My dark Rosaleen!

I could scale the blue air,
  I could plough the high hills,
Oh, I could kneel all night in prayer,
  To heal your many ills!
And one beamy smile from you
  Would float like light between
My toils and me, my own, my true,
  My dark Rosaleen!
  My fond Rosaleen!
Would give me life and soul anew,
A second life, a soul anew,
  My dark Rosaleen!

O! the Erne shall run red
  With redundance of blood,
The earth shall rock beneath our tread,
  And flames wrap hill and wood,
And gun-peal, and slogan cry
  Wake many a glen serene,
Ere you shall fade, ere you shall die,
  My dark Rosaleen!
  My own Rosaleen!
The Judgment Hour must first be nigh
Ere you can fade, ere you can die,
  My dark Rosaleen!

Attributed to OWEN ROE MACWARD
Trans. JAMES CLARENCE MANGAN

'The End.' Furlong's Irish Prayer Book, *1842*

Glossary of Irish Words and Phrases

(The standard Irish spelling is also given when it differs from the anglicisation in the text.)

a-gradh (*a ghrá*): darling
an eadh (*an ea*): is it?
Banbha: poetic name for Ireland
beoir: beer
coiblide (*caiblidí*): kind of colcannon
colcannon (*cál ceannann*): dish made of potatoes, cabbage, onion, milk and butter
Fódla: poetic name for Ireland
keen(e) (*caoin*): wail, lament
madder (*meadar*): wooden drinking-cup, 'mether'
merin (*múirín*): little wall, rampart
mo bhrón: alas!
pathereen (*paidrín*): rosary
ráth: earthern ring-fort or enclosure, rath
rinkafadah (*rince fada*): 'long dance', kind of traditional dance
scailtín: hot whiskey flavoured with other ingredients
shebeen (*síbín*): little tavern (which sells illicit whiskey)
skean (*scian*): knife
smachteen cron (*smachtín crón*): 'little brown mallet', a kind of tobacco
spoileen (spóilín, diminutive of *spóla*): small joint of meat
soogaun, sugaun (*súgán*): straw-rope
usquebagh (*uisce beatha*): 'water of life', whiskey

Acknowledgements

The editor and publisher gratefully acknowledge the co-operation of the following who have given permission for the reproduction of copyright material: Allen Figgis and Co. Ltd, Sandycove, Ireland, for 'A New Song on the Rotten Potatoes' (1847), from Georges-Denis Zimmermann *Songs of Irish Rebellion: Political Street Ballads and Rebels Songs, 1780–1900,* 1967; Associated University Presses, Cranbury, New Jersey, USA, for the poems 'An Answer to Thomas Barry' and 'Timoleague', both translated by Joan Keefe in *Irish Poems: From Cromwell to the Famine,* Bucknell University Press, 1977; Dolmen Press Ltd, Portlaoise, Ireland, for the poem 'On Christmas Day The Yeare 1678', from Diarmaid O Muirithe (ed.) *The Wexford Carols,* 1982; Gill and Macmillan, Dublin, Ireland, for 'Kerry Cows Know Sunday', from Daniel Corkery *The Hidden Ireland: A Study of Gaelic Munster in the 18th Century,* M. H. Gill and Son, 1925; Hamish Hamilton Ltd, London, UK, for the 'Letter from Skibbereen', from Cecil Woodham Smith *The Great Hunger: Ireland 1845–1849,* 1962; Irish Academic Press, Blackrock, Ireland, for extracts from John Dunton *Teague Land, or a Merry Ramble to the Wild Irish: Letter from Ireland 1698,* edited by Edward MacLysaght, 1982; Irish Texts Society, London, UK, for part of the translation 'The Satire of Domhnall na Tuile', from Rev. Patrick S. Dinneen and Tadhg O'Donoghue (ed.) *The Poems of Egan O'Rahilly,* 1911; Longman, Harlow, UK, for extracts from C. Litton Falkiner *Illustrations of Irish History and Topography mainly of the 17th Century,* Longmans, Green and Co., London, 1904; Oxford University Press, Oxford, UK, for extracts from *John Stevens: A Journal of My Travels since the Revolution (containing a Brief Account of all the War in Ireland, 1689-91),* edited by Rev. Robert H. Murray, 1912, and the poem 'This Night Sees Eire Desolate', translated by Robin Flower in *The Irish Tradition,* 1947; and A. D. Peters and Co. Ltd, London, UK, for the poems 'Last Lines' and 'Raftery the Poet', translated by Frank O'Connor (ed.) in *A Book of Ireland,* Collins Fontana Books, 1971.

Every effort has been made to trace copyright holders, but in a few cases this has proved impossible. The editor and publishers would be interested to hear from any copyright holders not here acknowledged.

Illustrations through the text have been reproduced from: William Carleton's *Traits and Stories of the Irish Peasantry,* published by William Curry, Dublin, in 1843; Mr and Mrs S. C. Hall's *Ireland: Its Scenery and Character etc,* reprinted in three volumes by Hall and Virtue, London, no date; a collection of Brian Merriman's poetry, published in Gaelic by Hodges and Figgis, Dublin, in 1912; Mrs Morgan John O'Connell's *The Last Colonel of the Irish Brigade,* published in two volumes by Kegan, Paul, Tench and Trubner, London, in 1892; Rev. R. H. Ryland's *The History, Topography and Antiquities of the County and City of Waterford,* published by John Murray, London, in 1824; Charles Smith's *The Antient and Present State of the County and City of Cork,* volume one, published by the author,

Cork, 1750; and *The Irish Sketch Book of 1843*, volume eighteen of *The Works of William Makepeace Thackeray*, published by Smith, Elder, London, in 1879.

Finally, the editor wishes to thank Rev. Desmond O'Connor S.J., Librarian of Newman College in the University of Melbourne, for his patience and advice.